The Long Shadow of
of
KATY'S KILLER

The Long Shadow of
KATY'S KILLER

Parole Hearings
and Other Updates to
A STRANGER KILLED KATY

William D. LaRue

CHESTNUT HEIGHTS

Copyright © 2025, William D. LaRue

The moral right of the author has been asserted.

All rights reserved.

No part of this publication may be reproduced, stored in a retrieval system, or transmitted, in any form or by any means, without the prior written permission of the publisher, nor be otherwise circulated in any form of binding or cover other than that in which it is published and without a similar condition including this condition being imposed on the subsequent purchaser.

Published by Chestnut Heights Publishing

ISBN 978-1-7322416-9-5 (paperback)
ISBN 978-1-7322416-7-1 (ebook)

Library of Congress Control Number: 2025901019

First edition. February 2025.

Contact the author at williamlarue.com

Front cover: The design incorporates Brian M. McCarthy's mug shot following his arrest in 1986.

Back cover (paperback): The design incorporates a photo of Katherine "Katy" Hawelka's gravestone at St. James Cemetery in Cazenovia, New York.

Copy editing: Kevin Hyland

Typesetting services by BOOKOW.COM

To my wife, Kathleen,
who has always made the impossible seem possible,
and has stood by me every step of the way.
With all my love and gratitude.

Contents

Foreword		1
1	The Mind of a Murderer	7
2	McCarthy's COMPAS	17
3	The Making of a Parole Appeal	33
4	A Family's Fight for Justice	45
5	McCarthy's 2021 Parole Hearing	57
6	The Good, the Bad, the 'Morbid'	75
7	McCarthy's 2023 Parole Hearing	85
8	'It's Never Going to End for Us'	129

Foreword

I parked my Nissan Cube outside Riley's, a popular restaurant in Syracuse, New York, on a beautifully sunny Friday in May 2018, just before noon. As I headed inside, a notebook tucked into a pocket, I wondered if I still had my reporter's knack for successfully pitching an important story. I was meeting Terry Taber and her lawyer, Joseph Fahey, who had invited me to lunch to discuss the email I had sent expressing my interest in writing a book about the decades-old murder of Terry's teenage daughter, Katherine "Katy" Hawelka. Soon, I was poking at my rib-eye steak salad, the greens barely getting a glance, as I made my case why I was the right person for this important and sensitive task.

In August 1986, I was working as a reporter for *The Post-Standard* in Syracuse when my father called with news that Brian Milton McCarthy had been arrested for a brutal attack on a 19-year-old sophomore at Clarkson University in Potsdam, New York. The Syracuse teen was beaten, strangled, and sexually assaulted outside the ice hockey arena as she walked to her campus apartment after an evening downtown with friends.

The crime hit close to home—literally. In the 1970s, McCarthy and I attended the same school, though we were several grades apart. He lived just a mile down the road, and I even babysat for his parents once. Back then, the McCarthys seemed like a nice, ordinary family, living the kind of quiet life that made people feel safe leaving their doors unlocked. It was impossible to reconcile the boy I remembered with the man who would later commit such a crime.

As we ate lunch, I explained how news coverage leading up to McCarthy's first parole hearing in 2009 had sparked my interest in writing a book to answer my lingering questions about the murder. Yet I also wanted to explore Katy's life and her family's fascinating fight to keep McCarthy in prison.

Terry listened quietly as I outlined my hope for interviews with her and Katy's siblings, their blessings to contact Katy's close friends, and access to family photos, court records, and other documents.

Terry met my gaze, her tone kind but resolute. Her primary concern was clear—that I might follow the pattern of so many true-crime books, focusing on the killer's troubled past while giving short shrift to the victim's vibrant life. She wanted the story to be told, but only if it encompassed the whole truth.

I assured her that was my goal as well. "I don't want to do anything that would add to the pain your family has already endured," I said.

As we wrapped up lunch, Terry said she would speak with Katy's siblings —Betsy McInerney, Carey Patton, and Joe Hawelka Jr.—and let me know their decision. I didn't say it, but I was prepared to thank them and move on if they said "no." I wasn't going to write the book over their objections.

Eight days later, on June 2, Fahey forwarded an email from Terry with the good news.

"It looks like we are onboard with this project," she wrote.

From that moment, I dove into the work, obtaining relevant police, court and prison records, collecting news clippings and TV news footage, and setting up interviews with Katy's family and friends. I tracked down Potsdam police officers who were on the force in 1986; the former St. Lawrence County district attorney who prosecuted the case; the president at Clarkson when the murder occurred; a former rescue squad volunteer who responded to the scene of the attack; and some of Katy's closest friends. Most agreed to be interviewed after verifying that Katy's family had approved.

I also reached out to McCarthy, requesting an interview in a letter I mailed to him at Riverview Correctional Facility in Ogdensburg, a city a few miles from Potsdam. I include the letter here, as McCarthy would later accuse me of pretending to be his friend to "trick" him into giving an interview. In it, I wrote:

> Dear Mr. McCarthy,
>
> I am writing to request an interview with you.
>
> You might remember me. I live now near Syracuse, but I grew up not far from you on Route 72 in Parishville and graduated

in 1975 from Parishville-Hopkinton Central School. I've been a journalist for more than 30 years, and spent much of that time writing for the Syracuse Post-Standard. I am now a producer with Advance Digital, which handles content for Syracuse.com and other sites.

I am interested in writing about what life is like for you in prison, about your daily schedule, what you do to occupy yourself and how you otherwise handle incarceration. I also would like to talk with you about your childhood and teen years and the events before you arrived in prison.

I have written quite a bit in the past about prison matters and I have always strived to write as accurately and as professionally as I can about criminal cases and incarceration. I would do the same for anything I wrote about you. I know a lot has been written about you in the past. However, I don't think I would know the complete story without talking to you personally.

I'd be happy to answer any questions you might have about this request if you write to me at the address...(with this letter).

If you (are) OK with talking to me for an on-the-record interview or interviews, I will proceed to set it up through Department of Corrections and Community Supervision.

Sincerely,

William LaRue

When he wrote back, McCarthy declined to be interviewed, stating he didn't want to "bring the pain back to the surface of so many who don't deserve to have that happen."

It took me more than two years to do the research and to write "A Stranger Killed Katy: The True Story of Katherine Hawelka, Her Murder on a New York Campus, and How Her Family Fought Back." The book, published in January 2021, triggered a fresh outpouring of public support for Katy's family. Thousands began following the family's Facebook page,

The Barnes & Noble bookstore in Clay, New York, prominently displays "A Stranger Killed Katy" in 2021. (William D. LaRue photo.)

4KatyHawelka, especially after national true-crime podcast "Morbid" devoted two episodes to the book. The podcast helped to boost to 60,000 the number of signatures on the family's **gopetition.com** campaign opposing McCarthy's parole.

For those unfamiliar with Katy's story, I recommend first reading "A Stranger Killed Katy" for a comprehensive understanding of her life, the details of her murder, court cases, and McCarthy's trouble-filled years before and after he went to prison.

Early chapters of "The Long Shadow of Katy's Killer" revisit McCarthy's first six parole hearings, aided by newly discovered court briefs, psychological reports, risk evaluations, and other documents. Later chapters dive into two new parole hearings, the family's media appearances, and the bright spotlight cast by the "Morbid" podcast.

This book provides an in-depth analysis of various documents, with extensive quotations in places. I initially worried that readers might find this approach excessive. However, I ultimately concluded that anyone engaged enough in Katy's story to pick up a second book would appreciate a deeper level of detail and insight.

In researching this book, I learned more about the significant role played by the woman identified in records as McCarthy's fiancée, an Upstate New York woman who is 14 years his senior. She has been instrumental in helping him to obtain independent psychological assessments, and in assisting with various other matters. However, she did not respond to my request for an interview. Given her low public profile, I am not identifying her by name.

I also reached out to McCarthy's longtime attorney, Cheryl L. Kates, but she declined to talk about McCarthy and her efforts to help him win parole.

"The Long Shadow of Katy's Killer" weaves old and new details in an attempt to create a compelling narrative that scrutinizes the prison and parole systems, tries to make sense out of a senseless murder, and chronicles relentless efforts by a grieving family to ensure Katy is never forgotten.

As you will read here, this story is still unfolding, revealing new insights and some enduring truths about the profound costs of a single, tragic morning in 1986.

— *William D. LaRue, February 2025*

Chapter 1

The Mind of a Murderer

LICENSED psychologist Joel H. Schorr left his office in Canandaigua, New York, on June 17, 2009, embarking on a 115-mile drive east along the Thruway toward Mid-State Correctional Facility in Marcy. It was a familiar journey, trading picturesque streets of his small town for the grim reality behind prison walls. His mission: to evaluate Brian McCarthy—a.k.a. inmate 87-D-0088—whose parole prospects could partially depend on Schorr's professional assessment.

After navigating the prison's layers of security, Schorr spent several hours with McCarthy, conducting an in-depth interview and administering a series of psychological tests. McCarthy had requested the evaluation, seeking a professional opinion that he wasn't at risk of reoffending if granted parole.

Three months earlier, following McCarthy's first parole hearing, the commissioners had enough doubts to vote 3-0 against releasing him.

"During the interview," the parole board told McCarthy in its written decision, "you demonstrate limited insight into your violent, heinous act and your remorse was superficial at best and geared toward ingratiating yourself with the panel. All factors considered, the panel concludes that your release at this time is incompatible with the welfare and safety of the community."

McCarthy, however, was not ready to succumb to despair. The next hearing, scheduled for April 2011, felt distant—but close enough that he knew he needed to start preparing. He pinned his hopes on Schorr's psychological evaluation, convinced that a favorable report could help to sway the next parole board.

For Schorr, a seasoned psychologist, the interview was yet another chapter in a long career dedicated to helping troubled individuals. In addition to

Brian M. McCarthy appears in mug shots, from left, for Potsdam Village Police in 1986, and for New York State Department of Corrections and Community Supervision in 2007 and 2017.

running a private practice in Canandaigua, he was a consultant for Clifton Springs Hospital, the Finger Lakes Alcohol Counseling and Rehabilitation Agency, the Ontario County Probation Department, and the Seneca Army Depot.

Schorr's accomplishments stood in stark contrast to the troubled life of McCarthy, then a 46-year-old convict with a rap sheet dating back to his teenage years. In the early 1980s, police in New York State arrested him multiple times, including for assault, burglary, petit larceny, possession of stolen goods, marijuana possession, and forgery. In 1985, Virginia police nabbed him for stealing a car, resulting in 10 months in prison.

McCarthy was on parole from Virginia on August 29, 1986, when he beat and sexually assaulted Katherine "Katy" Hawelka while the Clarkson University sophomore was walking alone on the campus in Potsdam, New York. Katy died three days later, and an autopsy found manual strangulation as the cause of her death. After McCarthy pleaded guilty a year later to second-degree murder committed during an attempted rape, St. Lawrence County Court Judge Eugene Nicandri sentenced him to 23 years to life, meaning McCarthy would not be eligible for parole until 2009.

At Mid-State, Schorr jotted notes as McCarthy attributed his criminal past to his abuse of alcohol and drugs, which he said stemmed from a trauma in his teens so horrific he couldn't talk about it for years.

Born in Connecticut on September 14, 1962, McCarthy grew up in the Upstate New York communities of Saranac Lake and Parishville. McCarthy spoke warmly about his parents, telling Schorr he didn't suffer any abuse at their hands. However, from ages 14 to 17, a "family friend" seduced and sexually molested him, McCarthy said. It was an experience he admitted he didn't disclose to anyone until "not too many years ago."

Schorr remarked that the molestation made McCarthy a "perfect candidate" for addiction and psychological difficulties. While he never received drug or alcohol treatment as a teen, McCarthy's parents arranged for mental health treatment several times.

"My parents tried to help me," McCarthy said.

McCarthy dropped out of high school following a "minor incident regarding a missing notebook that was, as far as he was concerned,…the last straw," Schorr noted in a six-page report, which became public in 2018 as an exhibit in New York State Supreme Court after McCarthy appealed a parole denial.

Schorr wrote that McCarthy had a "somewhat lengthy criminal history." Aside from the murder conviction, however, the psychologist listed only one other crime. By age 19, he noted, McCarthy had been arrested for burglary and marijuana possession—and Schorr left the impression that the court didn't take these offenses too seriously. "He served no jail time for either offense," Schorr wrote.

Schorr described McCarthy as having a "primarily positive record" in prison. His conclusion was at odds with records showing that McCarthy had numerous disciplinary tickets. This included a highest-level Tier 3 ticket just a few months earlier in 2008 after his state-issued razor went missing, a significant offense since inmates often used contraband blades as weapons.

Schorr stated that McCarthy provided personal history and other background used in the report. However, the psychologist said he realized it was important not to rely totally on reports of inmates. And so, Schorr said, he "made an effort to substantiate and compare reports of the inmate to the facts on record." Schorr did not specify what additional records he reviewed.

The American Psychological Association's guidelines for forensic psychology emphasize the importance of clearly documenting sources, methods of analysis, and the rationale behind conclusions. Such details are crucial for any parole board weighing the validity of a psychological evaluation. At a minimum, the parole board expected McCarthy to provide a truthful account of Katy's murder, seeing this as a critical measure of his accountability and rehabilitation.

In 1986, McCarthy admitted he ambushed Katy outside the Clarkson ice hockey arena, where he beat, kicked, and attempted to rape her while she was helpless on the ground. After he fled, two campus security guards spotted her lying unconscious and called the police. Officers found McCarthy huddled under a nearby staircase, complaining of back pain.

Hours later, in a taped confession to police, he made it clear that he didn't know Katy, that she never consented to sex, and that he tried at one point to "shake her insides out."

But to Schorr, McCarthy gave a much different story. He claimed that, after a night of drinking, he encountered a woman in "distress." McCarthy said he noticed that the woman "looked like she was sick and having problems."

"I had seen her before, and then I realized she was drunk," he told Schorr, whose report referred to Katy only as "the victim," never by name.

McCarthy recalled that the woman said, "I just want to have some sex." He further claimed, according to Schorr's report, "I couldn't perform. She laughed at me and spit in my face" and "I hit her."

"I remember hitting her, and she fell," McCarthy said. "I don't remember anything after that."

Schorr's report showed no effort to confront McCarthy about changing his story from his 1986 confession and his 1987 guilty plea. The report also didn't question McCarthy's claim he couldn't recall anything after striking Katy. Was McCarthy subconsciously blocking the truth from himself? Or was his claim of memory loss a fabrication designed to spare him from having to share the details of his crime? The report did not explore these questions.

Schorr stated that McCarthy "still at times can't accept that he committed this 'heinous crime and destroyed two families.'" The psychologist observed that "Brian's mood and presentation during this recounting of the instant offense was clearly unsettled and disturbed." Schorr continued:

> Brian states that he knows his crime is "heinous" and this appears to be a powerful motivational force pushing him to continue self improvement and self discipline. He feels that he understands and accepts his sentence and he also knows he has changed and is ready to be involved in society in a positive, lawful and redeeming manner. His 23 years in prison are additional regular reminders of his obligation to do so should he be given the opportunity.

Schorr's report continued by praising McCarthy's demeanor and intelligence:

> Mr. McCarthy was cooperative and talkative throughout the evaluation process. He spoke without hesitation and directly to the questions asked....He was adequately groomed. Eye contact was good. Thought processes were coherent and goal directed with no evidence of tangential thinking.
>
> Expressed self awareness and insight was at an average level. He was estimated to be in the very high average range of intellectual thinking. A lack of completed formal higher education effectively hides his intellectual power from the "naked eye." Throughout the interview and evaluation process Brian clearly and regularly demonstrated insight and positive attitudes in verbal and nonverbal ways. It is apparent to this examiner that Brian has rehabilitated himself and made a personal commitment to living a lawful and productive life in society should he be given the chance.

Schorr noted that McCarthy planned to live with his fiancée, a secretary near Watertown, New York. She provided Schorr with a letter supporting McCarthy's release, as did a former priest from Saranac Lake.

"Brian has been described as mature, sensitive and caring by a reverend as well as his [McCarthy's] significant other," Schorr wrote.

As part of the evaluation, Schorr administered several psychological tests, including the House-Tree-Person Drawing Test, the Shipley-Hartford Scale, the Level of Service Inventory-Revised, and the Sexual Violence Risk-20 Scale. Schorr reported that the latter two placed McCarthy at "low risk" for recidivism. The Shipley-Hartford "showed no signs of thought disturbances," while the House-Tree-Person found a "rehabilitated orientation." The psychologist added:

> It is apparent to this examiner that Brian has rehabilitated himself and made a personal commitment to living a lawful and productive life in society should he be given the chance....In this examiner's opinion he is clearly regretful for his actions....(and) it is the opinion of this examiner that he is not a threat to society and the individuals he would be in contact with upon release."

Schorr concluded with the statement: "Please do not hesitate to contact this office if necessary." However, on April 25, 2010, before McCarthy's next parole hearing, Schorr passed away at age 63 at his home in Canandaigua, according to his obituary.

By that time, Katy's family had seen McCarthy's transcript from the first parole hearing, so they were aware of his new claim that he injured Katy during a consensual sexual encounter. Her brother, Joe Hawelka Jr., was furious at reading this, stating that McCarthy was "soiling the memory of my sister" to secure parole.

New York prohibits the public from attending its parole hearings, so Katy's family must rely on transcripts, often released with large portions deleted to safeguard the privacy of inmates and others.

In their 2011 impact statements to the parole board, the family took aim at many of McCarthy's false statements from his 2009 hearing. However, because Schorr's report was confidential at the time, they were unable to review or challenge its conclusions.

On the afternoon of Tuesday, March 29, 2011, McCarthy attended his second parole hearing, this time at Marcy Correctional Facility, where he had recently been transferred. This time just two commissioners, Sally

Thompson and G. Kevin Ludlow, presided over the hearing, meaning McCarthy needed both votes to win parole. Ludlow had been familiar with McCarthy since 2009, when he met with Katy's mom, Terry Taber, and Joe Jr. to receive their impact statements.

At the 2011 hearing, McCarthy reiterated his claim that he accidentally killed Katy after she spit at him because he couldn't perform sexually. He also maintained he had once given her a free hockey ticket.

But while in 2009 he had denied having a previous relationship with Katy, McCarthy in 2011 had a different story.

"It is kind of hard to define 'relationship.' I did know her, and there was an intimate relationship with her prior to the night in question," McCarthy said. "But it was not something that was an everyday thing or week thing or month. Like I said, I had only known her a short time."

If the commissioners doubted McCarthy's truthfulness, or noticed how some details had changed from 2009, they did not say so.

The transcript made available to Katy's family showed no discussion of Schorr's report, although Thompson did praise the application packet prepared by McCarthy's attorney, Cheryl L. Kates.

"This is a terrible tragedy, no matter how you look at it from whatever perspective," Ludlow said of Katy's murder.

"It is very hard to live with, too," McCarthy said.

Shortly afterward, the commissioners voted 2-0 to deny parole, citing the "heinous nature" of the crime and McCarthy's "propensity for callous ...disregard for the sanctity for human life." The panel set McCarthy's next parole eligibility date for April 2013.

Before then, McCarthy would turn again to an outside psychological evaluation to bolster his case for parole.

New Jersey-licensed professional counselor Peter P. Buonocore paid a visit to McCarthy at Marcy Correctional Facility on October 5 and 6, 2012. Buonocore had agreed to evaluate McCarthy's "social, emotional, cognitive and adaptive functioning," and to prepare a report for the parole board assessing whether McCarthy posed a risk of reoffending.

In 2024, the New Jersey Division of Consumer Affairs listed Buonocore as holding an active license as a professional counselor for marriage and family therapy, effective October 5, 2012. Buonocore later remarked that it was a coincidence his license began on the date he began assessing McCarthy.

In his mid-50s, with a friendly face and soothing voice, the counselor was best known then as Maximilian Buonocore, a Benedictine monk at Newark Abbey. An online profile also described him as the guest master, kitchen master, and librarian at St. Benedict's Preparatory School in Newark. At the time, he was also studying for the priesthood.

Buonocore's 10-page report on McCarthy made it clear that his client left a positive impression. The counselor described McCarthy as "a single, 50-year-old Caucasian male, who looks somewhat younger than his stated age." He added:

> At the times of this evaluation, he appeared in appropriate and clean clothing, and was adequately groomed. Throughout the evaluation, he remained alert, compliant, adequately controlled and verbally responsive. During the interviews, he established eye contact with the examiner. Brian communicated using full sentences. His speech remained even paced, clear and sufficiently easy to understand. The content of his verbalizations in response to the examiner's questions was normally productive.

McCarthy's "strengths include good physical health, personal hygiene and care in appearance, as well as a good support system, and strong desire to work and be productive," the report stated, adding that:

> Brian's current hobbies are reading, cooking, jogging and Indian bead work. Other interests include building things, music, fixing cars/motorcycles, athletic activities, dance, fishing and hunting and other outdoor activities such as camping and hiking.
>
> During his 26 years of incarceration Brian has learned to be productive and has developed various skills. He has served as grounds keeper, worked in the areas of horticulture, construction, tailor shop, electrician, and has become a certified food

service instructor (cook). He has developed skills in air-conditioning, plumbing, radio and TV repair, and painting; and he works as a computer teacher's aide and a mobility assistant.

Buonocore quoted McCarthy's recollections of teenage trauma: "The sexual abuse I received was the primary factor to my maladjustment...to hide or dull those feelings."

McCarthy added, "I started using drugs, hanging out with the wrong crowd and acting irresponsible, engaging in violent conduct and venting my frustration for being abused."

Buonocore's report, like Schorr's, was often at odds with official records of McCarthy's criminal history, which began when he was a youthful offender, and continued from age 18 until the mid-1980s in New York State and Virginia.

The report incorrectly stated that McCarthy's criminal history began at age 19, and that McCarthy's nonviolent offenses "consists of two arrests for petit larceny, one of which included a charge of marijuana possession." Buonocore also said that McCarthy "has been free of any major disciplinary infraction while incarcerated these last 27 years."

Buonocore noted that he relied on background information provided by McCarthy's fiancée and handwritten notes from McCarthy himself. The report made no mention of what steps, if any, Buonocore took to verify information through court records, prison files, or other official sources.

Most notably, Buonocore did not report what McCarthy said, if anything, about killing Katy or if he denied trying to rape her. Buonocore did say there "is no evidence that Brian has engaged in extreme minimization or denial of past sexual violence."

The report never used the words "murder" or "attempted rape." It referred to the crime as the "offense for which he is incarcerated."

Buonocore screened McCarthy using several psychological assessments, including the Beck Depression Inventory-Second Edition, the Beck Hopelessness Scale, the Beck Suicidality Assessment Scale, the Beck Anxiety Inventory, the Sexual Violence Risk-20, the Hare PCL-R, and the Personality Assessment Inventory. The report noted that licensed psychologist Gerard A. Figurelli provided supervision and consultation.

The Beck tests indicated that McCarthy was not experiencing "clinically significant symptoms" of depression or anxiety, Buonocore wrote. However, he acknowledged that the Beck tests are "self-report measures," meaning their validity depended entirely on the honesty of the person being evaluated.

The Sexual Violence Risk-20, which evaluated the potential for sexual violence based on 20 risk factors, found no evidence that McCarthy had ever "suffered a sexual deviation, psychopathic personality disorder, major mental illness, or suicidal or homicidal ideation."

Buonocore's report provided limited details about the findings of the Personality Assessment Inventory, noting only that the results, combined with other data, reflected McCarthy's history of antisocial and offending behavior. The report did not disclose how McCarthy scored on the Hare PCL-R, a checklist of 20 traits and behaviors, including lack of empathy, superficial charm, manipulativeness, impulsiveness, and irresponsibility.

Buonocore concluded that McCarthy posed a low risk of reoffending, based in part on "his expressed responsibility, remorsefulness, and understanding of the consequences of his offending behavior." He wrote that McCarthy recognized and accepted "the nature and severity of his past offending behavior, its connection to emotional/behavioral maladjustment and substance abuse, and his awareness and acceptance that he requires ongoing help to enhance this resistance to relapse and promote his long-term adjustment."

One lingering issue for McCarthy, the report stated, was "a history of struggling with anger and learning to vent those feelings in appropriate ways." Buonocore noted that McCarthy completed an Aggression Replacement Training Program (ART) and the Sex Offender Counselor Treatment Program (SOCTP).

"Brian reported that he continues to apply skills that he learned from these programs, such as avoiding watching TV programs that include drugs and violence, and by practicing substitution techniques in which he engages in various forms of catharsis, including physical exercise, when he feels angry or feels like acting out his anger," Buonocore wrote.

However, a few months after Buonocore's evaluation, McCarthy's self-assessment shifted completely—suddenly, anger wasn't a problem at all.

Chapter 2

McCarthy's COMPAS

On February 22, 2013, as the wind howled and the temperature stayed below freezing in Marcy, Brian McCarthy sat inside, undergoing evaluation by the prison system's new computer software, COMPAS—short for Correctional Offender Management Profiling for Alternative Sanctions. The program collected data from an inmate's records and required him to answer a series of questions. It then generated scores to help assess the prisoner's risk of reoffending and to identify steps to reduce that risk.

Supporters of COMPAS argued that the software would enable parole commissioners to make decisions based on scientific data rather than guesswork or emotions. That's because the software was created using criminological research that identified traits and behaviors statistically linked to reoffending. An inmate found to have those factors during the COMPAS screening received higher risk scores in areas such as substance abuse, criminal involvement, emotional stability, and other issues.

However, the exact algorithm used to translate responses into scores was never disclosed. The developer, Northpointe Inc. (now Equivant), kept the formula a secret, leaving the parole board to rely on the tool without fully understanding how it worked.

The public was expected to have even greater blind faith. The New York State Department of Corrections and Community Supervision (DOCCS) considers individual COMPAS reports to be confidential. McCarthy's reports from 2013, 2015, and 2017 became publicly available as exhibits in 2018 when he took his parole denial to state Supreme Court.

In 2016, an article by ProPublica, an investigative journalism organization, questioned the transparency and fairness of COMPAS's scoring process, including the potential for flaws in how it evaluated risk. It also criticized the secrecy of the algorithm, which prevents external validation or scrutiny.

An offender rehabilitation coordinator at Marcy conducted McCarthy's 2013 COMPAS screening. The staff member answered the first 34 questions by providing answers about McCarthy's criminal history, his prison disciplinary record, his past substance abuse, his education, and his work history. Where the coordinator got the data was unclear, as his answers were sometimes at odds with known information about McCarthy.

For instance, Question No. 1 asked: "Was this person on probation or parole at the time of the current offense?" The staff member entered "neither," despite McCarthy being on parole from Virginia at the time he murdered Katy.

Question No. 14 asked: "Has this person ever received Tier 2 or 3 disciplinary infractions for fighting/threatening other inmates or staff?" The coordinator answered "no." However, Katy's family once obtained a detailed prison record for McCarthy showing he received a Tier 2 disciplinary ticket for fighting another inmate in 1989, another one in 1991 for telling a correction officer, "I'd love to kick your fucking ass," and one in 1996 for threatening an officer.

By 2013, McCarthy made it clear at parole hearings and elsewhere that his immediate family had little or no contact with him after his mother passed away in 2004. McCarthy would later acknowledge the last family visit he could recall was by two brothers around 2005, and possibly one after that.

But on Question No. 21, the coordinator checked "yes" that McCarthy's family "visited periodically during incarceration," that "inmate believes other relatives are supportive," and that he "intends to stay with family when released."

Question No. 22 asked: "Is there evidence of positive family support?" The staff member also answered "yes" to that.

If the coordinator considered McCarthy's longtime fiancée to be his "family," the report doesn't state this. The 2013 report lists McCarthy's marital status as "Significant Other." Later reports changed it to "Single."

COMPAS Question No. 19 asked: "Does this person appear to have notable disciplinary issues?" The screener answered "no," despite more than 14 disciplinary violations on McCarthy's prison record, including the Tier 3 ticket he received in 2008 for his missing razor.

Question No. 19 has a bad reputation among some parole-justice advocates. Former inmate Glenn Rodriguez alleged he was denied parole in 2016 because an offender rehabilitation coordinator at Eastern Correctional Facility answered "unsure" on Question No. 19, even though Rodriguez hadn't had a disciplinary infraction in at least a decade. Rodriguez complained that Question No. 19 was so subjectively phrased as to make it meaningless.

In 2024, the staff member who screened McCarthy was no longer available at his prison email address and telephone number, and he did not respond to other efforts to contact him.

For the next part of COMPAS, the coordinator asked McCarthy to answer 40 questions about social interactions, family support, finances, anger, and other issues related to his risk and rehabilitation needs.

The staff member began with a section that would be labeled "Self Efficacy" in the report.

"Please answer the following as either 'no,' 'yes,' or 'don't know,'" he said.

35. "Will it be difficult for you to find a steady job?"

"No," McCarthy answered.

36. "Will money be a problem for you when released?"

"Don't know."

The coordinator moved on to questions beginning with, "How difficult will it be for you to..." He instructed McCarthy to answer with either "very difficult," "somewhat difficult," or "not difficult."

37. "How difficult will it be for you to manage your money?"

"Not difficult."

38. "...keep a job once you have found one?"

"Not difficult."

39. "...have enough money to get by?"

"Not difficult."

40. "...find people that you can trust?"

"Not difficult."
41. "...find friends who will be a good influence on you?"
"Not difficult."
42. "...avoid risky situations?"
"Not difficult."
43. "...learn to control your temper?"
"Not difficult."
44. "...learn better skills to get a job?"
"Not difficult."
45. "...support yourself financially without using illegal ways to get money?"
"Not difficult."
46. "...get along with people?"
"Not difficult."
47. "...avoid spending too much time with people that could get you into trouble?"
"Not difficult."
48. "...avoid risky sexual behavior?"
"Not difficult."
49. "...keep control of yourself when other people make you mad?"
"Not difficult."
50. "...avoid slipping back into illegal activities?"
"Not difficult."
51. "...deal with loneliness?"
"Not difficult."
52. "...avoid places or situations that may get you into trouble?"
"Not difficult."
53. "...learn to be careful about choices you make?"
"Not difficult."
54. "...find people to do things with?"
"Not difficult."
55. "...learn to avoid doing things to people that you later regret?"
"Not difficult," McCarthy said.

For the next section, categorized under "Anger" in the report, the co-ordinator asked McCarthy to answer either "mostly disagree," "uncertain/don't know" or "mostly agree."

"How do you feel about the following?" he began.

56. "I feel other people get more breaks than me."

"Mostly disagree," McCarthy answered.

57. "People have let me down or disappointed me."

"Mostly disagree."

58. "I like to be in control in most situations."

"Mostly disagree."

59. "I will argue to win with other people even over unimportant things."

"Mostly disagree."

60. "When I get angry, I say unkind or hurtful things to people."

"Mostly disagree."

61. "I feel that people are talking about me behind my back."

"Mostly disagree."

62. "I feel it is best to trust no one."

"Mostly disagree."

63. "I prefer to be the one who is in charge in relationships with other people."

"Mostly disagree."

64. "I often lose my temper."

"Mostly disagree."

65. "I get angry at other people easily."

"Mostly disagree."

66. "I feel I have been mistreated by other people."

"Mostly disagree."

67. "I often feel that I have enemies that are out to hurt me in some way."

"Mostly disagree."

68. "When dealing with new people, I quickly figure out whether they are strong or weak."

"Mostly disagree."

69. "I often feel a lot of anger inside myself."

"Mostly disagree."
70. "I feel that life has given me a raw deal."
"Mostly disagree."
71. "When people are being nice, I worry about what they really want."
"Mostly disagree."
72. "When other people tell me what to do I get angry."
"Mostly disagree."
73. "I notice that other people seem afraid of me."
"Mostly disagree."
74. "I often get angry quickly, but then get over it quickly."
"Mostly disagree," McCarthy answered.

McCarthy's downplaying of his anger issues during the COMPAS screening sharply contrasted with his admission to Buonocore in October 2012, when he acknowledged ongoing struggles with his temper and described his efforts to manage it. His responses to the COMPAS questions suggest he changed his mind about having anger issues, or he approached the screening strategically, giving answers he thought would improve his scores.

In fact, a year before McCarthy's first screening, a New York parole officer claimed that many inmates were getting unfairly good COMPAS scores because they learned how to "cheat" the software. He said inmates obtained reports from each other, then answered with responses they saw from those who received low-risk scores, according to a February 12, 2012, story by the *Albany Times Union*.

"They're memorizing their answers," said the officer, who declined to give his name since he was not authorized to comment publicly. "So, the COMPAS instrument isn't going to be accurate."

Corrections spokesman Peter K. Cutler told the newspaper this was the first time he heard of inmates cheating on COMPAS. He defended the software as a "best-practices system to get them [inmates] back in the community and help reduce recidivism."

The developers of COMPAS also claim the software can detect efforts to fool the screening. But the report raised no red flags about McCarthy's honesty, stating, "No Potential Faking Concern" and "No Inconsistent Response Concern."

Risk Assessment

PERSON			
Name: BRIAN M MCCARTHY	Offender #: 04636359M		DOB: 9/14/1962
Race/Ethnicity: Other / Unknown	Gender: Male	Agency: NYS DOCCS	

ASSESSMENT INFORMATION			
Case Identifier: 87d0088	Scale Set: NY State Parole Risk (v. 3: Arrest, VFO, Absc)	Screener: ██████████	Screening Date: 2/22/2013 ✓

SCREENING INFORMATION	
Marital Status:	Significant Other
Prison Admission Status:	New Commitment
Prison Release Status:	First Parole this term/sentence

Criminogenic Need Scales

New York
- Risk of Felony Violence: 1 Low
- Arrest Risk: 2 Low
- Abscond Risk: 1 Low

Criminal Involvement
- Criminal Involvement: 4 Low
- History of Violence: 3 Low
- Prison Misconduct: 1 Low

Relationships/Lifestyle
- ReEntry Substance Abuse: 4 Probable

Personality/Attitudes
- Negative Social Cognitions: 1 Unlikely
- Low Self-Efficacy/Optimism: 1 Unlikely

Family
- Low Family Support: 1 Unlikely

Social Exclusion
- ReEntry Financial: 3 Unlikely
- ReEntry Employment Expectations: 2 Unlikely

A copy of Brian McCarthy's 2013 COMPAS report displays his risk scores calculated from data entered by a prison staff member and from answers supplied by McCarthy. (New York State Department of Corrections and Community Supervision.)

Not surprisingly, when COMPAS processed all the data, the software found McCarthy posed little risk of reoffending. It gave him scores of 1 or 2 that labeled him at low risk for "felony violence," "arrest," "abscond" and "prison misconduct." He also received scores showing he was unlikely to have "low family support," "negative social cognitions" and "low self-efficacy/optimism."

The only category it labeled as a "probable" risk was "reentry substance abuse," giving him a medium score of 4, despite McCarthy's claims he hadn't consumed drugs or alcohol since the morning he murdered Katy.

Given the overwhelmingly positive COMPAS scores, the parole commissioners might have anticipated that McCarthy would have nothing bad to say about the report when they interviewed him in 2013.

If they did, they were wrong.

On April 17, 2013, commissioners Edward Sharkey and Lisa Elovich met with McCarthy at Marcy Correctional Facility for his third parole hearing. Elovich noted this was her second time interviewing McCarthy.

After brief greetings and a review of the agenda, Elovich announced, "Let's talk about the reasons that you are in here. Very horrible crime."

Elovich read a summary in McCarthy's file noting the attack on Katy "took about 26 minutes from start to finish" and resulted in fractured fingers, numerous bruises all over her body, fractured larynx and broken nose, with the cause of death being asphyxiation due to strangulation.

"You said to Commissioner Ludlow during the last parole board interview—I read the transcript—that you had only struck Katy once and that she fell and hit her head," Elovich said. "That kind of is a slap in the face of what I saw in the file in terms of what her injuries were.... How could that possibly happen in one punch?"

"In a rage, in the process of a blackout," McCarthy answered.

"You are saying it could have been one punch?"

"It could have been more than one punch, more than one incident."

"From you?"

"From me," McCarthy said, adding, "It is pretty sad to know that I was capable of something like that."

"Could you imagine the fear and humiliation and horror that she must have felt during that time period?" Elovich asked.

"No, I can't."

"She did not die right away. She was put on life support August 29th... and taken off life support September 1st. Her family endured that period of time wondering whether she was going to make it."

"Pretty sad," McCarthy said.

"So, I did review your personal statement, also the sentencing minutes, talked about the plea," Elovich said, apparently referring to a checklist. "We do have your risk assessment form in the file, and it outlines your overall risk to the community as well as your criminogenic needs in the community. We'll consider that as well."

"Okay."

Elovich then asked McCarthy what he believed his greatest need would be under parole supervision.

Instead of answering directly, he referred to the COMPAS report and two psychological evaluations, both of which concluded "I am not aggressive behavior" and predicted a "low recidivism rate." Even then, he said, the risk assessments didn't convey the depth of his remorse.

"I think what the needs that they are looking at don't fill the needs of the sorry that I have," McCarthy said. "It is going to be one of the things that I am going to be dealing with, to be socially acceptable."

Elovich asked if there was anything else he wanted to tell the board.

McCarthy said he was "uneasy" that COMPAS rated him as "probable" for substance abuse and that he would need some kind of "drug rehabilitation."

"I have not done drugs in 27 years," he said.

Elovich said she thought the COMPAS score was based, in part, on how McCarthy blamed drugs and alcohol for his past troubles.

"[Y]ou did say that you were intoxicated and on drugs at the time you committed the instant offense and that also accounted for your past crimes as well, is that right?"

"I believe so, if that is the way they are looking at it," McCarthy said.

"The COMPAS risk assessment," Elovich said, "is…certainly not exact science. It is based on a lot of factors that are not tangible as well. The actual risk scores that they give, we'll give it the weight that it deserves as we do with every other factor that we are considering."

After the brief hearing, the commissioners voted 2-0 to deny parole.

In its written decision, the panel noted McCarthy's participation in prison programs, his letters of support, and his release plans.

"More compelling, however," Elovich wrote, "is the extreme violence you exhibited in the instant offense and callous disregard for the life of a young female college student, who you brutally killed."

She also noted significant community opposition to McCarthy's release. She didn't mention it, but the number of signatures on the Hawelka family petition opposing his parole stood at 5,851 just before the third hearing.

The panel told McCarthy he could apply for parole again in two years.

Commissioner Christine Hernandez greeted McCarthy on April 15, 2015, as he sat for a fourth parole hearing, once again at Marcy Correctional Facility.

"Good morning. How are you doing?" she asked.

"Good," he replied.

After introducing herself and Commissioner James Ferguson, Hernandez advised, "We are your parole board this morning."

She asked McCarthy, now 52, how long he had been in prison.

"This August will be 29 years," he said.

"What do you think about that?"

"I think I destroyed my life, as well as destruction of many other people."

Elovich asked McCarthy if he knew Katy.

"No, I didn't, not personally. I was aware of who she was, but I didn't personally know her," McCarthy said.

Then, perhaps recalling his claim from 2011 that they shared an intimate relationship, he casually amended his story. "I had a few interactions with her because of the facility campus. It was a college campus, and there was sports involved through a hockey game, and some of the people that I knew in the dorm and of the town knew who she was, and I knew she was on the campus, too."

"What were you doing on the campus?"

"Passing through."

After several minutes questioning McCarthy on his criminal and prison records, Hernandez turned to the psychological evaluations McCarthy arranged through Schorr and Buonocore.

"You also had been evaluated by a [redacted], right?" Hernandez asked, likely referring to Schorr.

"Yes."

"That was back in 2009?"

"There was a total of four, I believe," McCarthy said, possibly referring also to visits by Buonocore.

"Okay," Hernandez said. "But I am looking at the packet that you submitted in 2013, that was Mr. [redacted], and he goes through the whole thing, just saying the risk that he believes you pose. At this time, he doesn't believe that you pose any risk, right?"

"Exactly."

Hernandez wanted to hear McCarthy's opinion.

"Why do you believe you are a good candidate for parole?" she asked.

"All the years in prison, I see the guys come and go. I don't have that behavior anymore—the thinking capabilities, I don't have anymore. This is my change," he said.

"Where does the victim fit in?" she asked.

McCarthy wasn't sure how to answer.

"I was going to ask, 'Which victim?' There is more than one," he said.

It wasn't clear McCarthy was referring to himself, but the commissioner took his answer to mean that.

"Sir," Hernandez said, "you took the life of a young victim who had her life ahead of her. You took the life of one victim. You are in prison for that."

She repeated her question: "Why do you feel you are a good candidate for parole?"

Without trying to repair damage over his "Which victim?" answer, McCarthy spoke again about being a changed man.

"I have tried, everywhere that I have gone—I tried to do something productive," he said. "I have no misbehavior reports in seven years. I am not involved in drugs. I am not gang affiliated. I don't have any assaults or weapons. Everything I've done, I tried to be productive. College credits. I have multiple forms of credibility."

Hernandez turned to McCarthy's COMPAS scores from a screening on January 26, 2015, by the same staff member who conducted the 2013 one. The scores changed little from 2013. His score for "reentry financial issues" improved to a 2. The risk of reentry drug abuse was now a 6 and seen as "highly probable." McCarthy's drug score had been a 4 in 2013. This latest number bolstered the report's recommendation that McCarthy receive substance-abuse treatment upon release.

McCarthy said this score made no sense.

"I never had any involvement incarcerated with drugs," he said.

"You did this crime under the influence of drugs, though?" Hernandez asked.

"Yes, I did. But the risk assessment that was prior to this parole board hearing was a lower score," McCarthy said.

Hernandez suggested he might have answered questions differently in 2015.

McCarthy did not think so.

"It's a pretty standard format. It is the same way I answered this time. I know it is a new system that they are using. It didn't make any sense to me," McCarthy said before adding, "but I will participate."

McCarthy didn't explain why he was confident that he had answered every question the same as he did in 2013, especially given that he often claimed to have a faulty memory in many other matters.

After the hearing, the commissioners voted 2-0 to deny parole, and their written decision made it clear McCarthy had not done well in the interview.

Hernandez wrote that McCarthy "provided no reasonable explanation" for how his interaction with Katy led to her death. Furthermore, the commissioner was displeased by his response to a question about Katy.

"When asked about the victim, you responded, which one. A vibrant young woman was violently and deliberately assaulted and murdered. She is the victim, Mr. McCarthy, not you," she wrote. "Your entitled attitude leaves much to be desired."

The panel scheduled McCarthy's next parole hearing for April 2017.

On March 1, 2017, McCarthy sat for his third COMPAS screening, and the resulting report gave him scores mostly identical to ones from 2015, with a slightly worse one of 3 for the possibility of financial problems if released.

On the same day, the Marcy offender rehabilitation coordinator completed a Parole Board Report.

The coordinator read the following out loud to McCarthy and asked for his response:

> On 8/29/86 the Potsdam Village Police received a call from the Clarkson Campus Security at approximately 3:45 am, stating that they had discovered a girl who had been seriously assaulted and possibly raped. A patrol from the Potsdam Village Police responded as well as the local rescue squad. The arresting officer immediately responded to the Potsdam Hospital where the victim and the suspect (the subject) were taken by the rescue squad.

Clarkson University's Walker Arena is roped off on August 29, 1986, several hours after Brian McCarthy was arrested in his fatal attack on Katy Hawelka at the southeast corner of the building seen at right. Officers found McCarthy under the exterior stairs closest to the corner. (Potsdam Police Department photo.)

Based on the physical evidence at the scene, the subject was arrested by the police and charged with assault 1st and rape 1st. He was arraigned later on the same date. In the original information and complaint filed by the arresting officer of the Potsdam Village Police, he accused the subject of Rape 1st. He alleged on 8/29/86 at Walker Arena, on the Clarkson College Campus, in the Village of Potsdam, NY, at approximately 3:30 in the morning, the subject did engage in sexual intercourse with the female victim by forcible compulsion and without the victim's consent by reason of being physically helpless. The victim was beaten and kicked by the subject into unconsciousness, leaving her physically helpless. The grounds of this belief were the sworn statements of (Clarkson security guards) Kim Avadikian and Donald Shanty, the confessions of the subject, and physical evidence that was collected and preserved from the bodies of the subject and the victim.

> The victim of the rape was transferred from Canton-Potsdam Hospital to the House of the Good Samaritan in Watertown on 8/29/86 at approximately 2:26 pm. The autopsy was completed on the victim on 9/1/86 at approximately 8:00 and the final anatomical diagnosis showed evidence of manual strangulation. The subject was re-charged on 9/1/86 with murder 2nd.

When the staff member finished reading the summary, McCarthy's response, brief and measured, avoided addressing the graphic details:

> I know I can't change the instant offense. Being incarcerated 31 years has made me realize that other factors have changed. It has been a constant struggle to maintain all aspects of social acceptance. I can't imagine what the families directly involved have to deal with. I know the pain I caused will forever be felt. I am so remorseful.

To Katy's family, the statement was so typical for McCarthy—a stilted, superficial expression of remorse that focused more on his own struggles than on the devastating effects of his crime on Katy and others.

McCarthy's fifth parole hearing was scheduled for Tuesday, April 18, 2017, and Katy's family hoped to learn the decision later in the week. But that Friday when Katy's sister Carey contacted the Office of Victim Assistance, a staff member said it had no decision to share. Carey got the same answer when she called several times the following week, with no explanation for the delay. Katy's mother began to fear this was what happened when the board granted parole but wanted to hold off informing the victim's family.

Then, near the end of April, Joe Hawelka Jr. found a sympathetic staff member who confirmed the hearing had been postponed. McCarthy requested the delay while he appealed two disciplinary violations at Marcy Correctional Facility. According to Joe's source, the violations occurred April 7 when a sergeant filed a Tier 3 ticket for "harassment" and another for "threats."

On May 17, 2017, DOCCS transferred McCarthy to Riverview Correctional Facility in Ogdensburg where his appeal succeeded in wiping the violations off his disciplinary record. Even so, Riverview Offender Rehabilitation Coordinator Elizabeth Weir informed the parole board in a June 28 memorandum of the reason for the delay:

> Subject's reappearance in April, 2017, was postponed three months or earlier pending the results of a Tier 3 misbehavior report appeal....Subject appears appropriate for review by the July, 2017, Parole Board as the reason for the postponement no longer exists.
>
> Since his transfer to Riverview C.F. subject's institutional adjustment has been appropriate. Subject has not incurred further misbehavior reports.

On the morning of July 12, McCarthy's 2017 parole hearing finally got underway. This time, he sat in a room at Riverview, speaking via a video conference link with commissioners G. Kevin Ludlow and Marc Coppola at the parole office in Syracuse.

Before long, the discussion turned to McCarthy's COMPAS scores.

"The computer suggests in the COMPAS that, if on parole, you would present as a low risk to the public safety," Ludlow said. "What are your thoughts in that regard? Do you agree with the COMPAS, disagree?"

"I agree with the COMPAS," McCarthy replied. "I think that I am a low risk because I've tried throughout my incarceration to do everything I possibly could to rehabilitate the error that I made and the mistakes that I've also made in the institution....And I know the risk assessment that I had done is pretty consistent with the psychological evaluations that I had."

"When you use the word 'error,' are you referring to the assault and subsequent death of Miss Hawelka as an error?" Ludlow asked.

This time, McCarthy was quick to clarify his wording.

"I'm talking about my judgment, my error in judgment being that I was involved in a bad lifestyle," he said.

"I see," the commissioner said.

After a few more minutes of discussion, McCarthy pleaded to be allowed to "go home."

"Please see me as the person I am today and not as one who took someone's life almost 31 years ago," he said.

However, the commissioners voted 2-0 to deny him parole. They made it clear they believed McCarthy remained a danger. Coppola wrote:

> Following careful review and deliberation of your record and interview, this Panel concludes that discretionary release is not presently warranted due to concern for the public safety and welfare. The following factors were properly weighed and considered: Your instant offense in St. Lawrence county in August, 1986 involved murder second. Your criminal history includes larcenous and stolen property related offenses. Convictions in Virginia are also noted. Your institutional programming indicates progress and achievement which is noted to your credit. Your disciplinary record appears clean since your prior appearance.
>
> The Panel notes your COMPAS risk score of low; however, the Panel acknowledges official opposition and significant and persuasive community opposition on file to your release.
>
> Required statutory factors have been considered, including your risk to the community, rehabilitation efforts, and your needs for successful community reentry. Your discretionary release at this time would, thus, not be compatible with the welfare of society at large and would tend to deprecate the seriousness of the instant offense and undermine respect for the law.

The commissioners informed McCarthy that he could apply for parole again in April 2019.

But McCarthy didn't want to wait that long. Just days after this latest parole denial, he filed a notice of intent to appeal, initiating a process that would stretch on for well over a year.

Chapter 3
The Making of a Parole Appeal

To carry out his appeal, Brian McCarthy turned to Cheryl L. Kates, a lawyer from Fairport, New York, whom he had retained on and off since 2009 for parole matters. By late fall 2017, Kates had crafted a meticulous 32-page brief and delivered it to the parole board's Appeals Unit, demanding that McCarthy be granted a *de novo* hearing—a legal request to nullify the previous hearing and start anew.

She wrote: "This (July) hearing was not held in accordance to the laws regulating a Parole Board. The only remedy is to grant a de novo hearing so relevant information can be reviewed."

A longtime advocate for prisoner rights, Kates came to the practice of law after a short stint as a licensed practical nurse in the early 1990s, helping patients with brain injuries. After suffering a back injury that forced her to leave nursing at age 24, she earned a degree in 2002 from Syracuse University College of Law, where her passion for advocacy quickly took root.

"When you walk out across that (commencement) stage, where your mind-set is at the time, I was like, 'I'm going to change the world,' this and that," Kates said in a 2023 interview with "Hudson Mohawk Magazine," a radio news show airing from Upstate New York. "Then reality sets in. They don't teach you in law school that changing the world is a big job."

In 2024, Kates believed her law firm was the only one in New York State that restricted its practice to correctional matters. Her website contained numerous testimonials from former inmates she had helped to win parole. One was Cynthia Pugh, granted parole in 2008 after 24 years in prison for the shooting death of a roofing company executive in a Syracuse suburb. Kates also represented Terry Losicco, who won parole in 2016 after 34 years behind bars for beating a 67-year-old woman to death during a robbery attempt at her home in Westchester County, New York.

Over the years, Kates also supported pro-inmate legislation in Albany, and she worked to ensure the prison system implemented its own directives promising fair treatment. In a news release in 2019, she accused DOCCS of "official misconduct" by denying inmates access to official statements and community opposition letters opposing their parole. She complained this "veil of secrecy" hindered the ability of inmates to challenge erroneous information being presented to the parole board.

Although declining to be interviewed for "A Stranger Killed Katy," McCarthy in the summer of 2019 encouraged this author to report on Kates' complaints, which echoed some of his own concerns.

"I have retained a lawyer whom I would like you to put the corruption of the prison system in print for her," McCarthy wrote in a letter. "She is asking for the media to put the info out there....The state prison has many secrets the public would be shocked to find out, one of which is the records unavailable to everyone except the parole board."

DOCCS issued Directive 2014 on June 3, 2019, providing inmates with access to letters in their parole file from district attorneys and sentencing judges. The directive also allowed inmates to see letters of community support and opposition, if the writers' names were blacked out.

Speaking in general, Kates complained in a brief interview in 2019 that the appeals process was stacked against inmates, forcing them to undergo a burdensome and lengthy process.

"The system is still set up to keep prisoners in prison beyond what obviously they [the inmates] believe is fair," she said.

Kates noted that an administrative appeal typically takes four to five months to process, first with a review by the parole board's Administrative Appeals Unit, then by a panel of three commissioners. If denied at that level, she said, an inmate who seeks a review in New York State Supreme Court can expect it to take another year to get a decision. By then, even if the court orders a new hearing, there is no guarantee the decision will be any more favorable than if the inmate waited for the next scheduled appearance.

In New York State, an inmate could appeal a parole denial on several grounds, such as claiming the decision was arbitrary, lacked a rational basis, or ignored key evidence. Just because the inmate thought he deserved parole wasn't grounds to overturn the decision. The inmate needed to demonstrate that the parole board violated the law or failed to follow proper procedures.

In her November 27, 2017, administrative appeal, Kates questioned the integrity and competence of the commissioners who interviewed McCarthy.

"In the case at hand, the NYS Parole Board did not follow the statutory scheme governing how they make parole-release decisions," she wrote, alleging they used "unlawful procedures" and claiming their decision was "irrational bordering on impropriety."

Kates argued that the commissioners improperly cited "issues which took place over close to three decades ago." She claimed they "ignored and or not reviewed" the COMPAS risk assessment, and failed to "establish on the record" that they had discussed the psychological evaluations McCarthy and his fiancée had arranged.

The commissioners, Kates added, placed too much weight on McCarthy's past criminal behavior as well as current community opposition to his release. According to Kates, the board in denying McCarthy parole was, in effect, re-sentencing him. She wrote:

> He is being re-tried in the parole hearings. He is being re-sentenced according to the views of the Commissioners. He is being re-sentenced to de facto "Life Without Parole". He is not the same person he was entering the prison system as a young adult, many years ago.
>
> The Board reviewed factors based on the personal opinions of Parole Board members which is NOT an allowable factor for review....
>
> To hit Brian McCarthy at the Parole Board, is to alter his sentence and impose a term of "Life Without Parole" which is excessive. This is in violation of lawful procedure wherein the Board did not even review McCarthy's rehabilitative efforts as required. There is no rational reason to deny Parole.

Kates also attempted to carve out new legal territory by arguing that the parole board should grant McCarthy the same consideration typically reserved for juvenile offenders. She referenced the 2012 U.S. Supreme Court decision in *Miller v. Alabama*, which ruled it unconstitutional to sentence juveniles to life without parole for homicides without considering age and other mitigating factors.

Kates argued that, although McCarthy was 23 at the time of his arrest, he lacked the cognitive maturity of a fully developed adult. She wrote:

> Over the span of the last 15 years, scientific research and recent litigation brought to the fore-front legal issues pertaining to the development of an adolescent brain and the differences thereof when comparing the culpability of an offender over the age of 24 to that of a juvenile.... The mitigating factors of his [McCarthy's] age and decision-making process regarding brain development must be considered and it was not.
>
> He is much more capable of controlling himself as an adult. He matured while in prison. He is not the same man who committed the series of events which placed him in prison. He was capable of reform. He completed all recommended programming. He is sober.

Kates stated McCarthy had a "clean disciplinary record" over the previous 10 years. (She omitted any mention of the 2008 disciplinary ticket for the missing razor, or the tickets that had delayed his 2017 parole hearing while he successfully appealed them.)

About 10 weeks later, on February 8, 2018, a panel of three parole commissioners voted to reject McCarthy's request for a *de novo* hearing. The commissioners followed the recommendation of the Appeals Unit, which found no merit to any of Kates' arguments, including her claim McCarthy had been effectively resentenced to "life without parole." The unit pointed out that McCarthy was sentenced in 1987 to the indeterminate sentence of 23 years to life. This meant the judge left open the possibility he could spend the rest of his life behind bars.

"The appellate has not in any manner been resentenced," the unit wrote. "An inmate has no Constitutional right to be conditionally released on parole before expiration of a valid sentence.…Appellant's maximum sentence is life."

On March 13, 2018, Peter "Maximilian" Buonocore received a call from McCarthy, who had been transferred to Wyoming Correctional Facility in Attica, New York, the previous November. McCarthy's fiancée asked Buonocore to conduct another psychological evaluation, a task he accepted despite his busier schedule following ordination as a Roman Catholic priest in June 2017.

This time, Buonocore used the Substance Abuse Subtle Screening Inventory (SASSI-4), a tool designed to detect potential drug or alcohol problems. McCarthy hoped the test would counter the COMPAS finding he was "highly probable" to relapse into substance abuse if released.

In a six-page report, Buonocore concluded that McCarthy's risk of returning to substance abuse was "very low." However, the report was no slam dunk for McCarthy. Buonocore cautioned that, because of McCarthy's prior drug use, "the risk of future substance abuse cannot be ruled out" once he's out of the controlled environment of prison.

Buonocore's report also included results of his September 2017 administration of the Static-99R sex-offender risk assessment, which indicated that McCarthy was at low risk for future sexual violence.

The priest repeated his 2012 statement that he found "no evidence that Brian has engaged in extreme minimization or denial of past sexual violence."

Armed with Buonocore's report, Kates submitted it directly to Tina Stanford, chairwoman of the parole board, on April 30, 2018.

In an accompanying letter, Kates requested an immediate hearing so that a fresh parole panel could consider the SASSI-4 and Static-99R screenings, which she claimed DOCCS should have conducted prior to the 2017 decision.

"I am requesting a de novo hearing is conducted and this new relevant evidence is considered…that my client does not present a risk to the community," Kates wrote.

The parole board responded on May 22 that, after reviewing Kates' letter, it found no grounds to reverse its decision not to grant the *de novo* hearing.

Kates had noted in passing in her letter to Stanford that McCarthy was preparing if necessary to seek a review in New York State Supreme Court. On June 5, 2018, McCarthy did just that. Kates submitted an Article 78 petition to the court in Albany under the title *Matter of McCarthy v. NYS DOCCS*.

The arguments in McCarthy's petition seeking the *de novo* hearing mostly mirrored ones in his administrative appeal. In a signed affidavit, McCarthy contended that the board failed to consider mitigating factors such as his age and brain development at the time of the crime, improperly relied on community opposition, and ignored evidence of stable release plans, including housing and employment. McCarthy also alleged that the board did not properly consider his remorse and rehabilitative progress.

The state Attorney General's Office, representing the parole board, filed a 14-page response, which disputed each of McCarthy's claims.

The court file grew to more than 400 pages with exhibits that included many records never previously made public. They included McCarthy's COMPAS reports, his psychological evaluations, a criminal history for both New York and Virginia, his prison disciplinary record, his prison jobs dating back to 1988, and even the $425.25 added to his prison spending account in the prior six months.

On October 18, 2018, state Supreme Court Justice Andrew G. Ceresia found no legal reason to order a new hearing. The fact the parole commissioners were horrified by McCarthy's murderous attack was no reason to invalidate their conclusions, he said.

"While it appears that the Board placed emphasis on the gravity of the crime, it is entitled to do so," Ceresia wrote. "In that regard, the record reflects that petitioner's crime involved the sexual assault and brutal murder of a young woman. Under these circumstances, it cannot be said that the Board's decision evinces 'irrationality bordering on impropriety'."

Ceresia also determined that the hearing transcript contradicted McCarthy's contention that the commissioners had failed to consider his release plans or psychological evaluations.

"Petitioner also asserts that the Board relied upon erroneous and incomplete information, but he fails to identify any such information," the judge said.

As for McCarthy's complaint that the parole board should consider his age at the time he murdered Katy, the judge pointed out that "petitioner was 23 at the time of the instant crime and thus was not a juvenile offender entitled to special consideration of his youth and its attendant characteristics."

The court granted McCarthy one small victory: a reduced $15 filing fee, with no additional fees for the Article 78 proceeding.

By the time of the decision, it almost didn't matter. McCarthy's next hearing was around the corner anyway, this time at his newest residence: Cayuga Correctional Facility in Moravia, New York.

As McCarthy's sixth parole hearing unfolded on the afternoon of April 24, 2019, McCarthy continued his beef with the prison's computerized risk evaluation.

"There are a couple of things in this COMPAS that aren't accurate," he said not long after the hearing began at Cayuga Correctional Facility, this time with commissioners Tyece Drake and W. William Smith, along with Commissioner Marc Coppola, who was weighing McCarthy's fate for the second consecutive time.

McCarthy criticized the latest COMPAS report for raising his risk score to a 7 of 10 for reentry substance abuse, indicating he was "highly probable" for returning to drugs or alcohol if released. He considered the report so inaccurate "that I had written to my lawyer, and I had asked my lawyer if I could have this changed, and she said to write to the counselor. So, when I tried to write to the facility counselor, I got no response."

Aside from the substance abuse score, Coppola noted, COMPAS rated McCarthy favorably. The commissioner asked if he was disputing the positive scores, too.

"Just reentry substance abuse," McCarthy said.

Coppola glanced at the other numbers. He stopped at the positive score for family support, which he found surprising since McCarthy had acknowledged being estranged from his immediate relatives.

"I'm not sure I agree with that one," Coppola said of the score, adding that McCarthy's fiancée only would be "almost like family."

"She has written numerous letters on your behalf. That is support, maybe not actually family yet," Coppola said before reminding McCarthy that COMPAS was just one of many factors that go into the board's decision.

However, McCarthy continued to pick away at the report. He couldn't understand why some scores changed from one screening to the next. He worried the 2019 results were skewed by inaccurately stating he had moved from a "medium security" status to a "maximum security" one.

"I'll be honest with you," Coppola said, expressing some exasperation. "I've been doing this for a long time. We don't care what facility you're in. But don't waste time on that. I didn't know about it until you brought it up."

"Okay," McCarthy said. "But it does reflect the change in scores on my COMPAS."

Coppola said he had no idea if the prison's security status affected the COMPAS scores. Even if it did, he said, it was irrelevant to him.

"I don't focus on that. You are focusing on the wrong thing," Coppola said.

Coppola did want to talk about McCarthy's reasons for going to Buonocore and Schorr for psychological tests.

"Why the need to have the independent evaluations? Why did you feel that that was important, above and beyond the (COMPAS) risk and needs assessment that was created?" he asked.

The public transcript redacted McCarthy's immediate response before it quoted him as saying that "I also wanted to reaffirm what this COMPAS is really telling me the accuracy of being exposed to the prison system, has given me delusional thinking."

Exactly what he meant by that wasn't clear until, after another redacted comment, McCarthy seemed to suggest that he had sought outside evaluations to help correct his thinking.

"I know what I did. I could have corrective measures done, so I can never do this again, so I will have a fair chance of going to the parole board and getting a possible release," he said. "I'm trying to put a best foot forward, and if I can do that by having a counselor or psychoanalysis done, I can do

Brian McCarthy wears a bulletproof vest as he leaves a preliminary hearing on Friday, September 5, 1986, in Potsdam Village Court. Escorting him, from left, are Investigator Gene Brundage, Lieutenant Terry McKendree and Officer James Mason. Walking ahead of the group is Police Chief Clinton Matott. (The Post-Standard photo.)

that because I'm not a doctor, and I'm definitely not smart enough to do professional counseling, so if I can give someone the benefit of the doubt, I will do the best I can."

Coppola told McCarthy that the commissioners would consider the independent evaluations but not as a substitute for COMPAS.

Once again, McCarthy struggled to explain why his current version of the attack on Katy—that he struck her just once during a consensual sexual encounter—differed from his 1986 confession, when he admitted to ambushing Katy and brutally beating her.

McCarthy insisted he could no longer recall many details of what occurred that morning.

"I'm not avoiding it," he said. "I keep telling you, Mr. Coppola, I know what I did. I pled guilty to it myself and I'm ashamed of myself. I'm not the same person. You're asking me questions that I can't answer, and I'm trying.

If I can come up with answers that can satisfy you, they are the truth."

After the hearing ended, the commissioners voted unanimously to deny parole. They cited McCarthy's statements minimizing his violence inflicted on Katy, including his speculation that she died from asphyxiation because of the angle of her fall and "her neck was pinched."

The panel wrote that it considered the positive COMPAS scores, psychological assessments, letters of support, statements of opposition, and other factors. But "more compelling," the commissioners said, was the presentencing report describing a murder and sexual assault far more brutal than McCarthy was willing to acknowledge, adding that

> the gravity of your actions should not be taken lightly. Your victim was beaten and ultimately killed by your hand. During the interview, the Panel tried to gain more information and insight into your frame of mind, motivation and interaction with the victim, yet your explanation of how and why you were interacting with her lacks credibility. Furthermore, the Panel felt that you still have yet to fully and adequately examine your motives that led to this terrible crime, which remains a concern to the Panel.

The commissioners set April 2021 as McCarthy's next parole eligibility date.

By 2019, it was obvious, maybe even to McCarthy, that the board wasn't likely to grant parole if he stuck with a version of Katy's murder that clashed so starkly with his 1986 confession and 1987 guilty plea. His claims of selected memory loss also weren't cutting it.

How could the commissioners trust he was rehabilitated, or believe his promise to follow parole rules, if they suspected he was lying to their faces?

Yet he couldn't, or wouldn't, let go of this version of himself—the version that claimed a single, accidental blow had ended a life of a young woman he claimed wanted sex with him, a version clearly meant to cast himself as reckless but not monstrous. McCarthy had turned his actions from those of an attacker into a man wronged, a man who reacted in a moment of humiliation, with the unlikely story that Katy spit in his face because he couldn't perform sexually.

By now, the story was so entrenched that abandoning it would mean admitting he had repeatedly lied to the parole board, to others, and perhaps even to himself. Although doing so might help his chances to win parole, McCarthy refused to abandon his version, perhaps out of pride, perhaps hoping he would get a parole panel that failed to question it.

The result was a prison of his own making—one not constructed of concrete and bars but of words and memories distorted to the breaking point. McCarthy remained imprisoned by his own version of events so convoluted that even he struggled to keep the details the same from one hearing to the next.

After six hearings and six denials, McCarthy still had not given up hope. In May 2019, he filed another notice of appeal.

In her subsequent brief to the Appeals Unit, Kates repeated many of the arguments that proved unsuccessful in the past. She added this time that DOCCS had failed to provide McCarthy with copies of letters in his parole file, including ones from district attorneys, the sentencing judge, and individuals supporting or opposing his release. The Appeals Unit found no merit to this argument, noting that an agency directive to supply the documents didn't go into effect until June 3, 2019, more than a month after McCarthy's latest parole hearing.

Once again, the parole board declined to give McCarthy a *de novo* hearing, and no record could be found that McCarthy again sought a court review.

The June 2019 directive from DOCCS continued to deny inmates access to impact statements and other submissions from victims and their families. Records of meetings between families and parole board members also remained off-limits to prisoners.

But McCarthy didn't need those documents to learn what Katy's family said about him. Their anguish, outrage, and unyielding fight for justice was documented in detail in "A Stranger Killed Katy," a book that would eventually make its way behind prison walls after publication in January 2021.

Chapter 4

A Family's Fight for Justice

In early February 2021, Joe Hawelka Jr. tore open a letter from the Department of Corrections and Community Supervision. It was an invitation to deliver a victim impact statement ahead of Brian McCarthy's next parole hearing. This grim task was one that Katy's family had fulfilled every two years. But it always came with a price. As Joe had shared in "A Stranger Killed Katy," each statement felt like ripping the bandage off a wound that would never heal.

Since 2009, Katy's mother, Terry, and siblings Betsy, Carey, and Joe Jr. had presented their statements in person to parole commissioners. The death of Katy's father, Joe Hawelka Sr., in 2007 from non-Hodgkin lymphoma meant this bitter duty fell solely upon their shoulders.

The impact statements took months to prepare to ensure they carried the full weight of the family's grief and determination to keep McCarthy locked up. The family pored over parole transcripts, noting in their statements instances where McCarthy had lied, exaggerated, or changed his recollections from one hearing to the next. The family included photos of Katy, shared stories about her childhood, and documented the lasting impact of her murder.

But 2021 was unlike previous years. The publication of "A Stranger Killed Katy" had reignited public interest in their fight.

And then there was COVID-19. The virus had thrown a wrench into almost everything, including parole hearings. DOCCS suspended in-person impact statements. Instead, the state handed out phone numbers and access codes so families could call in and talk to a commissioner before a hearing.

Faced with these COVID obstacles, Joe vented in an email to his family that DOCCS should postpone everything.

"I personally think that even this process is far too dangerous in light of COVID and ALL hearings should be canceled indefinitely," he wrote.

Still, conceding the April 20 hearing would proceed whether he liked it or not, Joe scheduled his call with a parole commissioner for 9:45 a.m. on March 12.

The unsigned letter Joe received from DOCCS offered a list of potential topics for the meeting. They included:

- How your life has changed as a result of the crime

- The emotional and/or physical impact of the crime (injuries, long-term medical care, counseling, substance abuse issues)

- What has been lost (trust, jobs, money)

- Effect of the crime on children, other family members, friends, etc.

- Fear of harassment by the offender or others

- Any special conditions of release you would like to recommend to the Parole Board if a release decision is granted or if the inmate is approaching their statutory release date

- Any information that might not be in the case file

The letter assured Joe that a written transcript of the meeting would be provided to the parole board panel interviewing McCarthy. It also invited him to contact the Office of Victim Assistance with any questions.

Joe did so, later describing his conversation with a staff member as helpful. Among other things, he learned that, if McCarthy was released, the state would provide the family with contact information for his parole officer.

In early 2021, Katy's family launched a Facebook page, **4KatyHawelka,** to share parole updates and to promote media appearances. Betsy McInerney credited a daughter as the "technical guru" behind the page.

"My daughter Katy takes care of that," Betsy said in 2024. "Nowhere near do I have the ability to do that, so she handles it. She's named after my sister, and she's the one who keeps the page running."

The Facebook page prominently featured a photo of Katy Hawelka alongside a banner of daisies, her favorite flower.

The page's follower count grew from a few dozen initially to thousands as the months passed. The interactive nature of Facebook also provided a platform for supporters to engage directly, some sharing how they had written letters to the parole board or signed the family petition opposing McCarthy's release.

"I wrote a letter. My prayers to all of you," one follower commented.

In February 2021, Betsy finalized her impact statement and sent several photos to the parole board. One showed Katy posing with her sister Carey, both dressed for a prom. Another was Katy smiling for the camera just before returning to Clarkson for her sophomore year, still in a walking boot after a minor foot injury. A third photo, first published in "A Stranger Killed Katy," showed McCarthy at Canton-Potsdam Hospital raising a middle finger to a Potsdam police detective.

In a phone conversation with a commissioner on March 5, 2021, Betsy noted this was her seventh impact statement. She read aloud the following:

> My younger sister, Katy Hawelka, died as a result of injuries inflicted upon her in a brutal attack at the hands of Brian McCarthy. This is my opportunity to represent my sister who lost her life and ask that the inmate is denied parole for a 7th time.
>
> The inmate pled guilty to 23 years to life and I am respectfully asking the board to deny parole so that the inmate serves the full sentence of life in prison keeping others safe from the risk of another random act of violence in any community he could be released to.

> In the previous appearances seeking parole, he continues to be dishonest, lie and fabricate his story. My sister was on campus for a total of 10 hours when she was attacked. She was a victim picked at random and in each appearance, he still does not tell the truth, accept responsibility or even know her name.

Betsy condemned McCarthy's repeated claims that he struck Katy just once. Betsy wrote:

> There were 2 people at the scene. My sister was 5'7" and weighed only 140 lbs. at the time. To demonstrate how she really never stood a chance against this monster in a rage I submit a picture of the wristwatch that was cut from my sister's arm at the hospital. It [the band] measures a total of 3" in diameter.
>
> Through research I have learned that my sister never regained consciousness after she was strangled by Brian. I am submitting a copy of her autopsy report to demonstrate the extent of the injuries she sustained at the hands of Brian McCarthy....
>
> The brutality of the attack left Katy unrecognizable to my father when she arrived on a gurney to the hospital. Due to her injuries, my siblings and I were not allowed to see her in the hospital, as she was kept alive on life support.

Betsy's statement then shared how Katy's murder rippled through time and generations of family, affecting even those who weren't alive when it occurred.

> Fear and anxiety are a daily presence in my life today as a result of this attack on my sister. I am raising two college-aged daughters on my own.... The anxiety that I feel on a daily basis for my daughters' safety is solely based on the attack by Brian McCarthy on my sister.

Betsy offered a couple of examples of how phone calls or texts often leave her on edge.

One night in the fall of 2017, Betsy's daughter Katy was walking to her dormitory after basketball practice at St. John Fisher College when a car struck her on a street along the main campus. Betsy received a call around 10 p.m. from the basketball coach to say Katy was being transported to the hospital.

"The hardest telephone call in my whole life," Betsy told the parole board, "was to contact my mom on the frantic drive to Rochester and tell her about Katy. Well, by the grace of God, she did not sustain serious injuries, and her guardian angel aunt from whom she is named after was watching over her that day."

Betsy's second daughter, Molly, moved to an off-campus apartment during her sophomore year at St. Joseph's University in Philadelphia. Betsy initially felt Molly might be safer on campus. However, after a guard at the apartment building explained its safety protocols, Betsy agreed to the move, even though she worried Molly had to park on a street.

One night around 10:25 p.m., Betsy's phone rang. The caller ID showed the Office of Public Safety and Security. When Betsy answered, a university officer asked, "Are you the parent of Molly McInerney."

Betsy said she almost collapsed, regaining her composure only after the officer quickly explained the office wanted Molly to move her vehicle, which was parked too close to a driveway.

By 2021, when Molly or Katy called Betsy late at night, the first thing they would say was, "I'm okay" or "Nothing is wrong," knowing how much a simple phone call triggered their mother's anxiety.

As Betsy wrapped up her impact statement, she reflected on the countless milestones McCarthy had stolen from Katy and her family:

> Would we have a bigger family? Would she be living near me? Would we be raising our kids together? Would I be able to have coffee with her? Our family is like a puzzle now that doesn't have the last few pieces to complete it. Something is always missing. Katy and her hopes and dreams are missing. Brian McCarthy's ego-fueled rage took that.
>
> I will continue to fight on her behalf, today, tomorrow and every day forward from here. It will be my pleasure to provide a statement in 2023 and maybe, just maybe our family can have brief

moments of rest or peacefulness knowing that monster can never hurt another innocent human being for another 24 months and we continue to heal.

As the date for McCarthy's 2021 parole hearing neared, family attorney Joseph Fahey sent copies of "A Stranger Killed Katy" to Syracuse-area members of the state Senate and Assembly.

He included a 2019 essay he wrote for the *Albany Times-Union* that encouraged legislators to support Lorraine's Law, named for Lorraine Miranda, whose fiancé murdered her in Staten Island in December 1988. The legislation would allow parole commissioners to impose up to five years between hearings for inmates convicted of murder. Fahey argued this would ease the emotional toll on families faced with making impact statements every two years.

Katy's family members, Fahey wrote to legislators, "are forced to relive the horrible circumstances of her murder as well as express the pain and sorrow that they have experienced from her absence from their lives. I have appeared with them during some of these interviews and have witnessed the agonizing emotional toll these interviews and experiences take from them."

As of 2021, the legislation had stalled in the New York State Legislature after parole-justice advocates argued that Lorraine's Law could counteract reforms aimed at second chances for offenders who have demonstrated rehabilitation. Advocates also feared that a five-year gap between hearings would undermine efforts to address systemic issues like racial bias in the justice system.

Katy's family found far more success when it came to their efforts aimed solely at McCarthy. By early March, signatures on their online petition grew to about 8,100. As she did in the past, Carey planned to print out the list and include it with her statement to the parole board.

"This will be an awesome public campaign to make sure he [McCarthy] is denied parole at the hearing in April," Betsy wrote in a family email.

On Friday, March 19, 2021, Syracuse viewers tuning in WSYR-TV's public affairs show, "Newsmakers," watched as host Dan Cummings asked Carey Patton a question that cut to the heart of the emotional effects of giving impact statements.

The late Joseph Hawelka Sr. in a photograph that his daughter Betsy submitted to the parole board with her 2021 impact statement. (Hawelka family photo.)

"What's it like for you when you have to go before the parole board so frequently?" he asked.

Carey took a breath, her voice quiet and halting. "I will tell you this," she said, "that the time leading up to the appointment, usually several months before, we start thinking about what it is that we need to say. And so, I start reliving it. I know that Joey and Betsy and my mom start remembering all of the details, remembering all of the things that transpired so many years ago."

The program aired as a split screen—Carey, Joe Jr. and Betsy on the right, next to Fahey, sitting along a large, well-polished table in an office somewhere in the Syracuse suburbs. Cummings appeared alone on the left, occasionally holding up a copy of "A Stranger Killed Katy" and asking questions in the measured tones of a journalist careful to do his homework.

COVID quarantine rules kept the family and Fahey far from a Channel 9 studio. Instead, they spoke via a Zoom call, the sound echoing like it came from the bottom of a well, the video coming through washed out. (Due to Covid travel concerns, Terry wasn't able to be present.)

Despite its limitations, the interview was a rare and remarkable moment for local television—an in-depth glimpse into a family's grief and their unwavering case for keeping their daughter's killer behind bars. For the public, it was the closest they would come to witnessing impact statements firsthand.

Cummings began by introducing a photo of Joe Hawelka Sr. and invited Betsy to explain why she had shared it with the parole board.

"My dad was very reserved, a man of few words," Betsy said. "But you know, it is important that we mention that he's not here to speak on behalf of the family currently."

Cummings noted Betsy also presented the parole board with a photo of the gold-colored Pulsar watch that Katy was wearing at the time McCarthy attacked her. Returned to the family afterward and carefully preserved by Betsy in a jewelry box, the watch's band arrived broken, possibly from Katy trying to defend herself from punches and kicks. Betsy didn't rule out that someone cut it off in the ambulance or at the hospital while trying to save her sister's life.

In any case, Betsy said, the damage was a reminder of how Katy had to "fight a monster," and a symbol of what McCarthy stole.

"To me," she added, "it represents time, the time that you know she is not with us, the time that we've lost with her, the time that she's lost with our family."

For Carey, one challenge in meeting a parole commissioner every two years is that it means sharing intimate memories with a stranger, who in some cases comes to the meeting not knowing much about McCarthy or his criminal history.

"So, you're really trying to convince somebody who had no knowledge of my sister, no knowledge of what happened," Carey said. "And it's—it's very hard sharing these personal feelings with somebody who, who's just—it's a board. It's just somebody who has no vested interest in how it's affected our lives."

Joe Hawelka Jr. said one of the few rewarding aspects of delivering impact statements is the opportunity to call out McCarthy's lies.

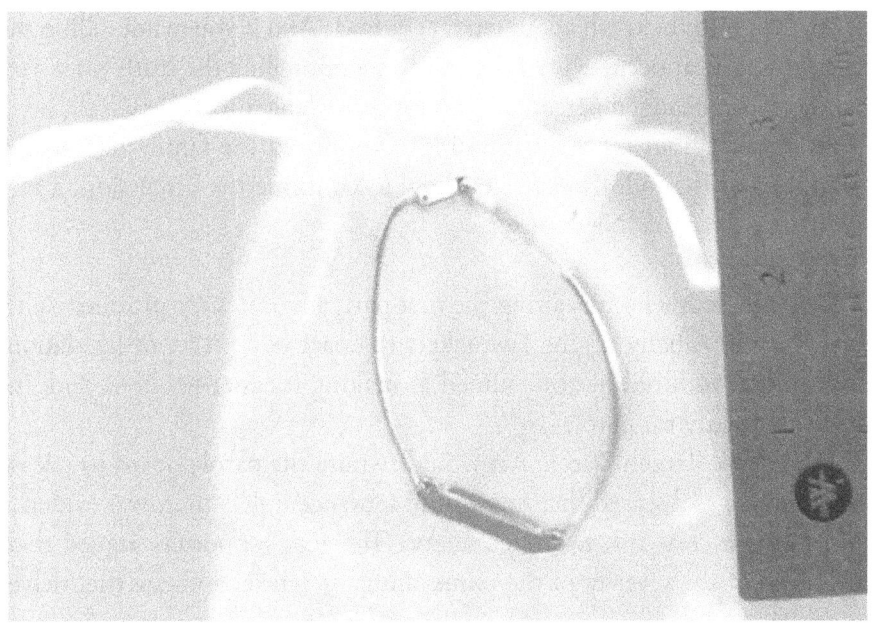

This is the gold-colored Pulsar watch Katy Hawelka wore on the morning she was fatally assaulted, with damage visible on the top right of the band. Her sister Betsy submitted this photo to the parole board with her 2021 impact statement. (Hawelka family photo.)

"He [McCarthy] has never not insulted the character of my sister, continuing to rob her of whatever grace she has," Joe said. "It's highly insulting to, you know, to read the minutes. But at the same time, it gives us something to address to the board in our next victim impact statement."

Cummings asked Fahey how McCarthy, despite pleading guilty to murder and attempted rape in 1987, could go now before a parole board and avoid "owning up to this crime in a real way."

Fahey, a retired Onondaga County Court judge, described McCarthy as someone who "in effect libels somebody in death" with his claims about Katy demanding sex and then instigating the attack. The parole commissioners have every right to judge McCarthy's lies as reason to believe he remained a risk to the community, Fahey said.

"We have an old principle in the law that says false in one and false in everything," Fahey said. "And that is a classic case of that here. He has never, ever told the truth about what occurred. And if you're not telling the truth about what occurred, you certainly are not telling the truth when you say...you're a changed person and no longer a danger to society."

As the first hour ended, Cummings announced the family had agreed to appear on the following week's show to continue the discussion, a rare two-part edition of "Newsmakers."

Even as Channel 9 was airing the first part, advocates for prisoner rights were busy in Albany urging lawmakers to enact two pieces of legislation, both first introduced in 2018, aimed at making it easier for New York inmates to qualify for parole.

The Fair & Timely Parole Act would require the parole board to release inmates who had served their minimum sentence unless there was evidence they posed a clear risk to public safety. The act's supporters argued that, regardless of the severity of the crime, inmates can rehabilitate themselves in prison.

Marvin Mayfield, lead statewide organizer with the Center for Community Alternatives, told *Spectrum News 1* in 2021 that the bill would prevent commissioners from imposing a "rubber-stamp denial" without giving "serious consideration what a person has done while they were serving their time."

During the second hour of "Newsmakers," Cummings noted that Fahey, in his essay in the *Albany Times-Union*, criticized the act for requiring "an undefined clairvoyance" on the part of parole boards by stopping them from weighing criminal history.

"I do think it could be guesswork at best," Fahey told Cummings, adding that prohibiting the consideration of a crime's horrific nature could open the door for release of notorious offenders like "Son of Sam" serial killer David Berkowitz or John Lennon's assassin, Mark David Chapman.

The second bill, the Elder Parole Act, would guarantee a parole hearing to inmates age 55 and older who had served at least 15 years of their sentences. Its supporters included former parole commissioner Barbara Hanson Treen, who in an essay for *The New York Times* argued the act was necessary because parole boards were "perhaps too cowardly" to grant parole when public opposition was likely.

"The parole board can simply decide that a parole applicant's release would, as the state's parole rules and regulations put it, 'so deprecate the seriousness of his crime as to undermine respect for the law.' Thus we have long-termers languishing through the years even though their risk of reoffending declines sharply as they age," Treen wrote. "For older people in prison, 'life' becomes just another word for a slow death sentence."

Fahey ridiculed the legislation's classification of 55 as "elderly," noting that even COVID vaccine eligibility initially defined elderly as 65 and older. He added that compassionate release programs already exist for inmates who become seriously ill.

"To suddenly make everybody eligible for parole at 55 regardless of what they did, simply because they've served 15 years of a violent felony sentence, to me it lacks any common sense," he said.

By contrast, Fahey said, Lorraine's Law was a reasonable option. The law would allow families of victims a five-year "breathing room" between parole hearings, he said.

Longer intervals also would provide parole commissioners with a "wider view of what, if anything, the inmate has accomplished in five years…(and) to make determinations about whether or not somebody has truly changed or reformed," Fahey said.

On Sunday, April 18, 2021, the *Watertown (N.Y.) Daily Times* published a front-page feature about Katy and about her family's efforts to deny parole to her killer. The newspaper accompanied the story with a sidebar on "A Stranger Killed Katy."

Clarkson University spokesperson Kelly O. Chezum told the newspaper that August 29, 1986, marked "the darkest day in the 125-year history of Clarkson University." Clarkson submitted a letter to the Board of Parole urging it to deny McCarthy's release.

"We submit," the letter read," that justice, and the physical safety and emotional wellbeing of our campus community, require that Mr. McCarthy be denied parole and that he serve the rest of his natural life in prison."

At his parole hearing two days later, McCarthy would make it clear he continued to view that darkest day in a much different light.

Chapter 5

McCarthy's 2021 Parole Hearing

By the time April 20, 2021, rolled around, Brian McCarthy had to feel a sense of déjà vu. Here he was back for his seventh parole hearing—another video conference linking Cayuga Correctional Facility to the Syracuse parole office. In attendance for his third hearing with McCarthy was Marc Coppola, a former state senator turned commissioner. The other commissioner present was Erik Berliner, formerly an official with the New York City Department of Correction.

By this point, McCarthy had spent 12,652 days incarcerated for the murder of Katy Hawelka, roughly 4,400 of which had passed since March 2009, when the parole board first denied his release.

Now 58, visibly graying and slightly heavier in a recent prison photograph, he was back in hopes of persuading a new parole panel that his remorse was genuine enough, his rehabilitation complete enough, and his explanations consistent enough to warrant release into society.

After his parole hearing in 2019, the board's written decision concluded that McCarthy's explanation of how and why he killed Katy "lacks credibility."

For this appearance, McCarthy had prepared a new narrative to convince the board he was telling the truth—he just needed the right opportunities to present it.

As the Tuesday hearing began, a stenographer again recorded every word, and DOCCS would again redact large portions from the transcript, making it difficult at times for Katy's family to fact-check what McCarthy said.

Commissioner Berliner took the lead in questioning.

"I need to go back to the beginning and get an understanding of what happened here in the first place, okay?" he said.

"Okay," McCarthy replied.

Reading from McCarthy's parole file, Berliner noted that the crime occurred at about 3:30 a.m. on August 29, 1986, on the Clarkson University campus.

"It says…you engaged in sexual intercourse with the female victim by forcible compulsion and then physically assaulted the victim. Is that true?" Berliner asked.

McCarthy responded, "That's what the statement says, but that's not exactly true."

Berliner asked McCarthy to explain.

McCarthy insisted that, while he did try to have sex with "this girl," he was unable to perform because "I was inebriated and under the influence of marijuana."

"Okay," Berliner said.

"And I—being that I couldn't perform," McCarthy continued, "she spit in my face and my reaction was to hit her, and it was an instantaneous reaction. Was it intentional? No. It was a spontaneous act, and I regret it, but it wasn't something that I had planned."

Despite redactions, it's clear McCarthy then blamed being sexually molested for triggering his substance abuse and anger issues.

"And being under the influence—I don't know if you have ever been under the influence of drugs and alcohol, I hope not—but being that I have been clean for almost 35 years, I have come to realize that [redacted] my reasoning was way out of whack [redacted]….I was a little bit angry at the world and that anger came out."

"Let me ask you a couple of questions," Berliner said. "How old were you?"

"Twenty-three."

"Okay. What were you doing out at 3:30 in the morning?" he asked.

"Out drinking, just having fun, partying."

Berliner inquired if McCarthy was a Clarkson student. McCarthy said he wasn't but lived nearby.

"The victim here," Berliner asked, "did you know her previously?"

"Yes, I did."

Berliner wanted to know how.

McCarthy stated he had seen Katy on campus "during certain events" in her freshman year. He frequented the dorms "because I'm a local and knew a lot of people there."

It was here in the hearing, as evidence he knew Katy, McCarthy mentioned an incident he never previously told a parole board: She had been carrying her cousin's photo ID.

"There was a discrepancy on the identification," he told the commissioners.

"A Stranger Killed Katy" had disclosed from police records how officers briefly misidentified Katy as her 21-year-old cousin because Katy was carrying the cousin's Elmira College ID.

Without claiming he had read the book, McCarthy brought up that confusion to try to explain why police in 1986 thought he denied knowing Katy.

"And the police officers asked me as they held up the ID to my face and asked me if I knew her, and I said, 'No,' because her ID was not her ID," he claimed. "She had someone else's identification because she was underage, and she was out drinking with an ID that was able (to allow her) to drink."

"Okay," Commissioner Berliner responded neutrally.

McCarthy pressed on, insisting the ID mix-up had been "a discrepancy that's been going on for years," even admitting he had never addressed it before.

Again, Berliner's response was a flat, "Okay."

McCarthy didn't offer details on when or where officers supposedly showed him the cousin's ID card. Police records show no such instance, or why they would even think it necessary to show a victim's ID to the suspect.

Even if they had, that wouldn't explain why McCarthy never told them when shown the ID, "That's not Katy," or why he never mentioned knowing her during two police interrogations. It also didn't explain why he conceded at sentencing in 1987 he didn't know her prior to the attack.

After reading the 2021 transcript, Katy's sister Betsy said she had no doubts at all that McCarthy fabricated being shown the ID, in hopes of persuading the parole board he wasn't lying about knowing Katy.

"Of course, McCarthy got the mistaken ID information from the book," she said.

Berliner and Coppola didn't pursue the ID story, perhaps realizing it didn't in any way prove McCarthy knew Katy.

"Well," Berliner said, "let's try to be a little specific in this case. Did you know her name?"

"Yes, I did. I knew—at the time, I knew of her first name. I didn't know—I knew she lived on campus, but I didn't know her last name."

"Okay. Had you ever dated?"

"No."

"Had you ever had a conversation with her?"

"Yes. There was a conversation," McCarthy said, proceeding to repeat a story he gave at past hearings about how he had tickets to a Clarkson hockey game in 1985 and gave Katy one so she could attend. (Katy's family and friends have disputed this, noting she wouldn't need a ticket since Clarkson students received free admission to games.)

McCarthy conceded their relationship wasn't close enough to exchange greetings in public. "But to say, 'Hi, how are you doing?'—it wasn't like that."

"Yeah," Berliner said. "And you didn't consider the ticket to the hockey game a date, right?"

"Absolutely not," McCarthy said.

"All right. I think I understand. Had you ever had sex with her prior to the night?"

"No, absolutely not."

Berliner summarized McCarthy's claimed relationship: "Okay. A very casual, 'I know who you are, I know your first name' kind of thing?"

"Right," McCarthy said.

"She knew your name, or she just knew you as Brian?"

"I think she knew me by Brian."

"Okay," Berliner said.

"I had a nickname that was, like, part of my last name as Mac, but some people knew me as Mac, but it was—"

"But she would have known you somewhat casually as this guy around town or this guy on campus?" Berliner asked.

"Right, absolutely," McCarthy said.

As Berliner continued questioning, it was clear he still had trouble believing McCarthy's claim that Katy agreed to have sex outdoors at 3:30 a.m.

"So, you are walking across campus, and you bump into her, or you went looking to see her?"

"No, I was walking across campus," McCarthy said.

"Okay."

"And I happened to see her."

Berliner noted that, in his own college experience, such encounters didn't typically lead to someone saying, "Hey, let's have sex."

"I don't know how to explain it. It's country living," McCarthy said of Potsdam. "It's not that big of a college. I'm familiar with the area. I know a lot of people in the town. I have a very well-to-do family and a very big family, and there was a lot of family that were very familiar with people that went to college there."

Berliner tried to redirect McCarthy's answers to his encounter with Katy.

"I understand how you bump into somebody on a college campus. What I'm getting at is—and I don't want to put words in your mouth, so if I misunderstand you, let me know."

"Right."

"But the way you described it earlier, this began as a consensual sexual relationship, yeah?"

"Yes, absolutely," McCarthy said.

"How did you get from 'We barely know each other's name; we've never spent any real time together,' to 'bumped into each other at 3:00 on campus and we are about to have sex'? How did that happen?" Berliner asked.

"She was inebriated and so was I, and the consensual thought was—" McCarthy began.

Berliner stopped McCarthy there.

"I'm sorry," the commissioner said. "I don't mean to interrupt you. She was walking alone? She was with friends?"

"She was alone," McCarthy said.

This contradicted a portion of McCarthy's 1986 confession that he had spotted Katy walking and talking with a male friend. After the man left,

McCarthy said, he circled the hockey arena, ambushing her along one corner before punching, kicking, and attempting to rape her.

Since McCarthy was now offering a different version, Berliner pressed him for details.

"So, she's walking across campus; you are walking across campus," the commissioner said, attempting to summarize McCarthy's story. "You say, 'Hey, [redacted], it's Brian,' or Mac or whatever and then you started talking?"

"I don't know," McCarthy said. "I don't really remember how that went, but it was kind of like, you know, it might have been something social."

McCarthy speculated that he might have asked Katy, "Are you on your way home?" or "Are you going back to the dorm?" Her response, he said, was "kind of, like, 'How are you doing?' or 'What are you doing?' or, you know, and 'I'm not doing much.'"

McCarthy paused, seeming to acknowledge the vagueness of his recollections.

"I don't—35 years ago, man," he said.

The commissioners said nothing, so McCarthy continued.

"It just went to the point where you just meet somebody, you know, that's a good-looking guy, and she was a good-looking girl, and it was, kind of, like, you know, we are both inebriated, let's have some fun."

"Okay," Berliner said.

McCarthy added, "No strings attached."

"Okay. Fair enough," Berliner said. "Where did this first take place?"

"It was behind the hockey arena," McCarthy replied.

Berliner asked, if the encounter was consensual, why didn't they go to Katy's dorm apartment or to his place.

McCarthy said he didn't realize Katy lived on campus, and his own place was too far away.

"It wasn't convenient," he said in an explanation that doesn't account for the fact Katy certainly knew she lived nearby.

"Okay. All right," Berliner said. "So, you begin to have sex. You said you couldn't perform—this is, I'm assuming, alcohol- and drug-related failure to perform?"

"That is right."

"She got angry and spit in your face?"

"Yes."

Berliner asked why Katy would spit at him.

"Because I couldn't perform, and she was laughing, and I think that being that I was under the influence of drugs and alcohol and [redacted] it all piled up," McCarthy said. "I mean, you are not in your right frame of mind when you are inebriated or under the influence of drugs, and my instantaneous reaction was to swing or physically lash out."

"Okay. All right. And you strangled her, right? That's, ultimately, how she died?" Berliner asked.

"Yes," McCarthy replied, though he quickly qualified his statement, adding that he wasn't entirely certain about how Katy died. "I hit her, and I admitted that I hit her, and she fell."

"Okay," Berliner said.

"And being that she fell," McCarthy said, "I think it was written that there was head trauma or there was trauma, I don't know, it's been a while since I have reviewed the medical reports."

With that, McCarthy sprang on the board another story he never previously mentioned at a parole hearing. This one involved DNA.

In 1986, Potsdam police had plenty of evidence to charge McCarthy with rape. Katy had been found beaten and unconscious, wearing only a sweater and blouse, both yanked above her chest. Two Clarkson security guards had seen the attack and, at first, mistook it for a couple having sex because McCarthy was on top of Katy, his pants down. When the police arrested McCarthy, they spotted what looked like blood on his clothing and boots.

The medical staff at Canton-Potsdam Hospital administered a "rape kit," combing Katy's pubic area for foreign hairs, using swabs to collect bodily fluids, and taking blood and saliva samples.

If the case had gone to trial, the lawyers would've brought out the forensic results. But it never got that far because McCarthy pleaded guilty to murder committed during an attempted rape.

McCarthy told Berliner and Coppola that the proof he didn't rape Katy was the fact tests didn't find his DNA.

"I even asked about the DNA for the rape, and they said, 'There was no DNA.' So, I was like, 'Well, how can the charge of rape be included in that?'"

By claiming his DNA wasn't found on Katy, McCarthy was making an argument that scientific evidence was on his side.

However, it would have been impossible for anyone to tell him there had been "no DNA." In 1986, the New York State Police Crime Laboratory, which served the Potsdam police, was years away from using DNA analysis of crime scene evidence. Instead, forensic analysts examined the rape-kit swabs for the presence of seminal fluid. Had they found any, they would have tested it for blood type markers to determine compatibility with McCarthy. They also would have conducted microscopic comparisons to match McCarthy with foreign hairs and clothing fibers collected from Katy.

The commissioners said nothing about McCarthy's DNA story.

He then claimed that he pleaded guilty to attempted rape because it seemed like the right thing at the time.

"You know, so I ended up pleading guilty because I knew what I did," McCarthy said. "If there was that much violence, you could say that I attempted to rape this woman. If that's the way that it reads, I'm not an idiot. If that's the way the violence was, if I was that out of my mind and I was that inebriated, you know, I'm taking responsibility for what I did."

"Okay," Berliner said.

McCarthy said, "I'm trying to be as truthful as I can."

"I have not sensed you holding anything back. I appreciate that," Berliner said.

"Okay. Thank you."

The transcript heavily redacted Berliner's next exchange with McCarthy, but it appeared to center on how an ambulance transported McCarthy to Canton-Potsdam Hospital after the police found him under a Walker Arena stairwell complaining someone kicked him from behind.

Berliner wondered if Katy hit McCarthy, or if he got hurt some other way.

"Did someone try to break up what was going on here? Or did you get drunk and fall? Or do you not remember?" Berliner asked.

"No, she didn't hit me. Somebody might have hit me, I don't know. I could have fallen. I'm not saying that I didn't, but I'm not saying that I did. I don't remember that part," McCarthy said. "And I've (been) hit before and it, kind of, blanks things out."

Berliner didn't press McCarthy to explain why he changed his story from 1986 when he eventually admitted to the police that he ended up under the stairs because he struck his head on "the railing or something."

Berliner turned to McCarthy's criminal history before Katy's murder, including arrests for petit larceny, burglary, and drug possession, as well as a 1985 prison stint in Virginia for stealing a car.

"You described yourself, when you and I first started discussing this, from a well-to-do family. What's with all of the larcenies?" Berliner asked.

"Because I was mischievous. I was into smoking marijuana and being the—you know, I don't know what you want to call it,…"

The transcript redacted the rest of his comment. But from his follow-up remarks, it's clear McCarthy again mentioned being molested as a teen.

"And I was afraid to say anything to anyone because this was a well-to-do person of the community, a respected person of the community, and he actually raised my father. So, he had very close ties with my father," McCarthy said. "And it was, kind of, fearful as a young kid, I was in my early teens, that if I said something what kind of repercussions. They're not going to believe me."

"Right," Berliner said.

"So, my avenue was to vent by going out and being mischievous just to get away because I was frustrated," McCarthy said.

"I'm sorry that happened to you," the commissioner said. "I know that's really bad that it happened. You never disclosed this at the time, right? It's only recently that you have made that clear?"

"Right, absolutely right," McCarthy said.

Berliner turned to McCarthy's time in prison in Virginia. He asked McCarthy if he was on post-release supervision at the time he murdered Katy.

McCarthy expressed uncertainty.

"I want to say that there was a possibility that I was still on a probationary term," he said.

Berliner then pointed out that records in McCarthy's file show that indeed he was on probation.

"Right. I think it was still interstate compact. Is that how they explain it?" McCarthy said, revealing familiarity with how New York agreed to supervise him after his release from a Virginia prison in 1985.

The commissioner noted McCarthy's record was free of recent disciplinary offenses, indicating "inside (of prison), you have adapted, fair to say?"

"I believe I have," McCarthy replied.

Berliner also pointed out McCarthy had completed several prison programs, including ART (Aggression Replacement Training) and Oneida Correctional Facility's sex-offender therapy.

"That actually opened up a lot of windows for me because they are really good counselors," McCarthy said of the Oneida program. "They took the initiative because I was kind of standoffish. I didn't really want to get involved because I was kind of fearful of what I might find out. And being that I found out that some of the skills that I needed to address, one of them was fear, but also looking at it as where that was probably one of the first times that I have admitted…"

The transcript redacted the rest of his sentence, but it appeared McCarthy referred again to his childhood molestation.

McCarthy said that "opening up like that, it's pretty scary." The prison system, he added, tended to foster "being tough, 'don't admit that,' you know, and hiding behind a shield."

After Oneida counseling, he said, "I look at things in a real way. I don't have any hidden agendas that I believe that I used to hide behind. So, when these counselors gave me the opportunity, who were very professional, and said, 'You need to deal with this. Otherwise, you are going to be running from it for the rest of your life,' that's what I learned to do…to deal with it in a sense of the program's needs and the program's tools."

His positive assessment contrasted with his comments at the 2019 parole hearing, where McCarthy criticized the Oneida program as unhelpful, claiming staff ostracized and mistreated him. McCarthy didn't explain this change of heart in 2021.

Berliner brought up McCarthy's COMPAS assessment, which rated him as low risk for "violence, arrest, and absconding" if paroled but showed a higher risk for "reentry substance abuse."

"You feel like when you go home, you'll be able to maintain your sobriety?" Berliner asked.

McCarthy replied that he had avoided illegal substances for nearly 35 years in prison, despite their availability among inmates.

"I have no desire to be involved with any alcohol or drugs," he said. "I can't emphasize to you how good I feel. I'm healthy, my frame of mind, my body, and knowing that I see guys in here and the destruction it does and the involvement they have with drugs, and I just shake my head. It just blows my mind to know this is what I'm destined to if I start using drugs. Why would I want to do that?"

Without waiting for another question, McCarthy returned to his longtime criticism of COMPAS, complaining that in 2021 it gave him a worse risk score of 7 for "reentry substance abuse," compared with a 4 previously.

"I didn't do anything different.…I didn't have (drug) tests that were positive, and I have been urine tested," McCarthy said.

Berliner explained that COMPAS scores were partly subjective, based on the inmate's answers to questions and a counselor's observations, in addition to criminal and substance abuse history. He indicated that the board placed more weight on high-risk scores for violence than for substance abuse.

"Then we can put that (substance abuse) risk aside and not be too concerned about it. Does that make sense?" Berliner asked.

"It absolutely makes sense," McCarthy said.

Berliner asked about McCarthy's parole packet and his "case plan" for life after release, including strategies to avoid drugs, manage stress, and handle finances, employment, and other tasks.

"Talk me through your plan. How are you going to make it work?"

"I've paid my dues. I try to look at (situations) in a positive frame of mind. If it's negative, I get away. If I don't have the opportunity to get away, I try to use my vocal skills."

McCarthy described his approach for handling difficult situations: He might tell other inmates, "Listen guys, I don't really want to be around this.

I think it's better that I—don't get mad at me, please. I'm going to step away."

McCarthy added that he regularly called a priest, apparently referring to Father Buonocore. The priest gave him "insight and hindsight so that I don't have to fall back on the wayside, and keep growing and learning on more tools. Not just with praying and walking away from stuff, but how to communicate with people."

Berliner asked how long McCarthy had been with his fiancée.

McCarthy replied, "It's got to be 18 or 19 years, maybe."

Berliner joked, "You're going to hear about it then when you have to struggle to figure out how many years you have been together, you know that, right?"

"Don't say that," McCarthy said.

Berliner noted the fiancée "writes a nice letter on your behalf," one of at least three people to do so for this parole panel. McCarthy said the fiancée was a senior administrative secretary at a college.

"She's worked there for—I'm going to get this wrong too, but I think she's been there for 28 years," he said.

"What about you? How are you going to support yourself?" Berliner asked.

"I have a lot of skills," McCarthy said. "I worked on a farm when I was (a) youth. I have pretty good mechanical skills. I have some very extensive electrical skills. I'm pretty knowledgeable about mechanical, and I'm not afraid to get my hands dirty. I have some really good farming skills."

In prison, he said, he worked on the "garden squad" building flower beds and growing other things.

"I'm not above working in a barn, you know, shoveling cow manure; it wouldn't bother me a bit. If I have to work wherever to make a dollar legally, I will do whatever I have to do, because I'm really looking forward to making my debt to society on the outside."

McCarthy added, "I hope I can be given a chance."

With that, Berliner said he had just one "big section" yet to cover with McCarthy.

"But I want to pause for a second here to see if Commissioner Coppola has any questions," Berliner said.

Coppola, mostly silent until now, wasn't finished with McCarthy's claim of knowing Katy before the murder.

"You said you had saw her the year before on campus?" he asked.

"Right," McCarthy said. "It was in a dorm setting where the campus has the dorm rooms, and I used to go to the dorm rooms because I knew a lot of the students that were at the college campus. So, I used to frequent the college campus and, being that I was a local, I had access to marijuana, and I used to go on the campus and smoke marijuana with some of the students."

Coppola asked whether any others ever confirmed to McCarthy that they knew he was acquainted with Katy.

"Oh, I don't know. I couldn't answer that question."

"Did you talk to her at all?"

"There might have been innocent communication," McCarthy said, recalling she was with a group one time he offered hockey tickets.

"That was the first time you ever saw the victim?"

"I believe that's pretty accurate."

"So more like a casual in passing, kind of?" Coppola asked. "There was no, you know, conversation with her. It was in passing, is what you're saying?"

"Directly communicating to her, no, I don't think that was part of the scenario," McCarthy said.

Coppola asked if the attack on Katy occurred a year after he gave her a hockey ticket.

"It might have been a little bit more than a year, I think," McCarthy said, adding that on dates and years, "my brain is not that sharp."

"We will say several months. It wasn't a day or two later, or it wasn't three weeks later?" Coppola asked.

"No, no."

"It was a while?"

"Yes, it was quite a substantial time later."

By the time Coppola passed the questioning back to Berliner, McCarthy's evasive and inconsistent answers had thoroughly undercut his claim of knowing Katy prior to the morning he murdered her.

"When you pled guilty, were you promised a particular sentence?" Berliner asked.

"No, I was not," McCarthy said.

Berliner was referring to McCarthy receiving 23 years to life in 1987. The sentencing transcript showed Judge Nicandri gave McCarthy two years less than the maximum to reward him for pleading guilty and giving up his right to a trial. Defense attorney Charles Nash also asked the judge for a slightly leaner sentence.

Berliner hadn't been clear, based upon the sentencing transcript, if there had been some kind of plea agreement.

"I can tell you that my lawyer spoke up during sentencing," McCarthy said, "and he said he would recommend to the judge, which really doesn't mean much, 22, 23 or 24 to life."

"Right," Berliner said.

"That was my defense lawyer, so if that has any credibility of what you're trying to get to—"

Berliner interrupted.

"I'm not trying to get to anything," he said testily. "I'm saying Judge Nicandri, on the record, explained what his thought process was about you pleading guilty and sparing everybody trial and the mitigation of your substance use, right?"

"Yes," McCarthy said.

Berliner's questioning also had clarified that McCarthy knew that a sentence of less than 25 to life didn't mean that the judge had downplayed the severity of the crime.

In fact, Berliner said, in the small community of Potsdam, the murder of Katy was "the crime of the century."

McCarthy didn't disagree. But the comment stirred in him a bitter memory of his 2015 parole hearing with Commissioner Christina Hernandez, who was no longer with the parole board. Hernandez had severely admonished him after one of his answers left her believing he considered himself the victim.

"I know that it was very bad," McCarthy said of the impact his crime had on the community. "I tried to explain this through a commissioner that had resigned, and I tried to express to her that I realized the pain that was caused and the families that were hurt. And she went off the deep end, and I never got the chance to explain to her that I was talking about all of the other people that were involved, not just direct blood family. I'm talking about the family that she went to school with, I'm talking about the community that supported all of the colleges in the area, and I'm talking about my family."

Berliner and Coppola said nothing as McCarthy continued.

"There's some of my family that I've never spoken to because of this. They refuse to speak to me. They refuse to acknowledge my existence. It's pretty mind-blowing to know you can do something like that and have that kind of a negative impact," McCarthy said. "How do you resolve the hurt or the pain or the corruption or the disruption that you have started in life? How do you come back and resolve that? Is it ever resolved? I don't think so."

Once again, McCarthy had turned a discussion of his crime into a lament about the impact on himself.

Berliner was puzzled by the suggestion that McCarthy was still trying to understand his actions and how to make amends.

"If you can't resolve what you did," the commissioner asked, "why are you and I having a conversation at all?"

"Because I'm looking for answers," McCarthy said. "The answers that I need to go on with what I'm trying to do in life to redeem whatever qualities I have left. If those are the answers I need, maybe you can help me, maybe you can't. There's still a few things that are unanswered in my mind. One of them is: Am I ever going to be forgiven? Probably. Will this ever be forgotten? I don't think so because I know I'll never forget."

"Right," Berliner said.

McCarthy continued, "I know that it was a terrible crime. I know that some of the people that I hurt will never, ever recover from the pain."

Berliner reminded McCarthy that he had gone to the wrong place if he thought the commissioners were there to absolve him of his sins.

"Sometimes I think there's a misapprehension about what we do here. The Board of Parole is not where you go for forgiveness, right?"

"No," McCarthy said.

"This is a question about release or denial," Berliner said.

"Right."

"And it's not my role, nor would I ever deem to forgive, or not, your behaviors. We are supposed to make an impartial judgment under the law, and that's what we are going to do."

Berliner asked McCarthy to share his thoughts about Katy Hawelka.

"The thing we haven't talked a lot about in the time we have spent together so far is" Katy, the commissioner said. "I know a little bit about how you knew her, and I know from the file how her life ended, but I don't know what you think about that today."

"To think about her as a person?" McCarthy asked.

"Yeah. Well, the life you took."

"Speaking specifically, I mean, any life in general, but speaking specifically about her, it's sad that I did that to her," McCarthy said. "It's sad that she ended her life in a way that she didn't have any control over, and I also look at it in a sense of as the years went on, I found out that she was a really good person, and it's almost sad that I'm still alive and she's not."

To Katy's family, reading the transcript later, McCarthy's clumsy choice of words—"she ended her life" and "it's almost sad"—offered startling proof about his lack of rehabilitation. Even in 2021, he had trouble owning up to what he did or offering full remorse.

McCarthy continued, "After all of the turmoil, all of the chaos, her family still suffers, but she doesn't suffer anymore because of me. That's pretty selfish. That's pretty selfish on my behalf, and not to have the opportunity to live out her life. She was looking for a higher education. She won't have that opportunity anymore. So, if the blame can be put on someone, I've already admitted to my guilt, and the blame should be put on me."

McCarthy didn't say who might put the blame for Katy's murder on anyone other than himself.

"Whether someone looks at it as I'm a piece of garbage, it doesn't matter to me," he said. "It's something I have to deal with because I caused her life to end, and I'm very ashamed of the cause of that. I know that a lot of other people directly related to her had a lot of physical conditions because of her death, and whether it was dying from a sad heart, a broken heart, that was because of me. I'm not running from that."

McCarthy didn't say who in Katy's family died of a broken heart. None of them ever claimed that.

As he continued in another partially redacted exchange, McCarthy spoke of how he had turned to counseling to help "deal with something like that."

"Where do you start? How do you come to a resolution? Where do you actually take your mind in here?" McCarthy said. "In this setting, in this prison setting, where do you take your mind to let your guard down to give some kind of resolve knowing that you caused so much pain? How do you do that? And I'm getting the answers. I am getting some of them. I hope that I get a chance to do it in the street. It will be more of a private setting, but if not, I will have to deal with it."

After allowing McCarthy to talk uninterrupted for several minutes, Berliner began to wrap up the hearing.

"You have answered all of my questions," he said. "We have spent a good amount of time together. I feel that I got to know you a little bit."

McCarthy pleaded with the commissioners to see he was "not the same person" he was when he killed Katy.

"I hope you take into consideration that I'm asking for a chance, and that if it's feasible, that's all I can ask," he said.

Berliner told McCarthy to give the commissioners "a few days to go through all of it, okay?…There's a lot to consider here. We will get back to you with a decision. Good luck."

Three days later, on Friday, April 23, Joe Hawelka Jr. took a break from work to call the state's Office of Victim Assistance in hopes it had a parole decision. A staff member took a moment to check records before sharing the news: "He was denied."

The board decided McCarthy would not be eligible for his next hearing until April 2023.

That was all Joe Jr. needed to hear. He hung up and immediately made phone calls to his sisters, his mother, and family attorney Joseph Fahey.

"I am starting to tear up, and I don't know why," Joe Jr. told his mother as he shared his unexpectedly emotional reaction to the good news.

"It's relief," Terry explained quietly, herself now in tears. "We got two more years. At least he's in for two more years."

On June 17, the family received a copy of the unanimous decision.

"In light of the low risk COMPAS and your good disciplinary record, the Panel does not find you to be a significant risk for future criminal behavior," Coppola wrote. He also praised McCarthy for his "personal growth, programmatic achievements and productive use of time."

On the other hand, Coppola noted that McCarthy had been on probation supervision at the time he murdered Katy, a crime that "had long-lasting impacts on the victim, her family, the university at which it occurred and the town."

Coppola also made it clear the commissioners viewed McCarthy's answers as an effort to minimize his crime. The panel "found that, while you were able to express regret for your actions and some significant growth, you also displayed limited remorse for your victim and her lost life specifically."

Katy's mother, Terry Taber, although pleased by the denial, was somewhat troubled by the wording of the decision. She questioned how the commissioners could state that McCarthy wasn't at significant risk for future criminal behavior, a finding that removed one barrier to McCarthy's eventual parole.

"This is why we have to continue to fight his release," Terry wrote in a Facebook post. "Why it is so important to send letters and get people to sign the petition against his release in 2023. Please help. It is more crucial every time he goes before the parole board. Thank you, Katy's mom."

But even as members of Katy's family were thinking ahead to 2023, they were unaware McCarthy wasn't yet done fighting for parole in 2021.

Chapter 6

The Good, the Bad, the 'Morbid'

In the spring of 2021, Brian McCarthy spent much of his time working under the designation of "facility maintenance painter" at Cayuga Correctional Facility. But as he acknowledged at his parole hearing that April, the painting part was just a technicality—an official job title for a task new to the prison. The truth was that he was on the frontline of the COVID-19 epidemic. Equipped with cleaning supplies, he diligently scrubbed and sanitized the S-Block cells, a critical task in the medium-security prison. By February 2021, approximately 180 inmates, or about 27 percent of the prison population, had tested positive for the virus.

Despite the unglamorous nature of the work, McCarthy approached it with purpose, viewing it as a chance to learn a new skill.

"My job title and my skills that I was given to clean, direct contact with COVID-19 in S-Block—it was a learning skill, it was a learning curve that I did want to have," he told the commissioners at his April hearing.

When he wasn't cleaning or visiting the law library preparing for his next parole hearing, McCarthy said, he liked to jog, keeping himself fit physically in a place where it's never good to look weak.

"And I look at it in a sense that I pray, I work out, I run," he said. "I'm almost 60 years old, and I go out and I run a couple of miles three, four times a week. I'm in pretty good shape for an old man."

In the month after his latest parole denial, McCarthy set his sights on one other task: filing another administrative appeal. On September 8, his attorney, Cheryl L. Kates, submitted the paperwork, mostly repeating arguments that had gone nowhere in earlier efforts to win a *de novo* hearing.

She contended that the parole board's 2021 decision improperly deviated from the COMPAS assessment that showed McCarthy at low risk of reoffending. Kates argued that the parole board denied release based solely on the seriousness of the offense; that the decision was "conclusory" and lacked detail; and that the board improperly resentenced McCarthy. She also repeated that the parole board failed to consider McCarthy's youthful age at the time of the crime.

The parole board's Administrative Appeals Unit—in a response a bit harsher than the hearing commissioners' written denial—found each of these arguments to be without merit. It pointed out that the hearing transcript showed that Berliner and Coppola based their decision on proper evidence, reasoning, and statutory guidelines. The unit added:

> In reaching its conclusion, the Board permissibly relied on the instant murder offense, which was committed while on supervision and which represented a severe escalation in the Appellant's criminal behavior, as well as the Appellant's lack of remorse for the victim's loss of life....The interview transcript reflects that the Appellant displayed limited remorse for the life of the victim and continued to focus on consequences he has faced.
>
> Inasmuch as Appellant contends the Board failed to consider requisite factors, there is a presumption of honesty and integrity that attaches to Judges and administrative fact-finders....The Board is presumed to follow its statutory commands and internal policies in fulfilling its obligations.

The Appeals Unit delivered its most pointed rebuke by citing as precedent *In the Matter of Brian McCarthy, NY Sup. Ct. Index No.: 3664-18 (2018)*, McCarthy's failed Article 78 proceeding, and how the judge rejected the notion that a man nearly 24 years old when he murdered Katy should be treated like he had been a juvenile offender.

Citing McCarthy's own failed case served as a deliberate and emphatic reminder that this argument had already been thoroughly reviewed and dismissed by a court of law. The citation in a public document had a side benefit for Katy's family of alerting them to the Article 78 proceeding and its many exhibits.

The Good, the Bad, the 'Morbid'

After reviewing the Appeals Unit's recommendations, parole commissioners Ellen Evans Alexander, Tana Agostini, and Caryne Demosthenes voted 3-0 in November 2021 to uphold the April denial.

After that, McCarthy resumed his routine of cleaning cells, working out, and spending time in the Cayuga Correctional Facility's law library preparing for his next hearing in 2023.

In May 2022, Terry Taber heard that a Massachusetts-based national audio podcast was streaming a two-part episode focusing on Katy, McCarthy, and "A Stranger Killed Katy." With a mix of curiosity and caution, Terry clicked on a link to "Morbid: A True Crime Podcast," a show previously unfamiliar to her.

For the next hour, she listened as hosts Alaina Urquhart and Ashleigh "Ash" Kelley presented their candid and unfiltered account titled "The Horrific Murder of Katy Hawelka."

Urquhart described the case as "crazy," and she informed listeners she would later share details on how to support the family's petition opposing parole for "the man who was responsible for these crimes."

Alaina Urquhart, left, and Ashleigh "Ash" Kelley are the hosts of "Morbid: A True Crime Podcast." ("Morbid" publicity photo.)

77

"I'm going to sign it," Urquhart said. "I think once you guys hear what he did, you are going to want to sign it too, and I really urge you to. But obviously, listen for yourself, right? I think you'll come to the same conclusion."

"Morbid" stood out as an ideal platform to rally public support for the petition, given its widespread popularity and devoted listener base. By the time the first episode about Katy's murder premiered on May 9, "Morbid" was on numerous lists of the most popular podcasts in the United States.

Urquhart and her niece Kelley launched the podcast in 2018, offering irreverent commentaries on famous crimes, horror stories, and weird events. (They affectionately referred to their fans as "weirdos.")

Urquhart, with her background as an autopsy technician, brought a forensic perspective to the podcast, while Kelley, a hairstylist, contributed a relatable, everywoman perspective. They often injected dark humor and a few vulgar words into their commentaries, and yet they still made sure to show empathy and respect for victims and their families.

"This family really fights for Katy's legacy," Urquhart said in introducing the first episode about her murder. "They fight for justice, and I really give them a ton of credit for putting themselves out there constantly and fighting for this."

Kelley added, "The fact that they have to go before the parole board every 24 months…and just basically beg for him not to be let out. He's an animal, in my opinion. He deserves to be behind bars for the rest of his life."

To prepare this episode, Urquhart said, she twice read "A Stranger Killed Katy," and followed it up with her own research. She was happy to read a true-crime book that emphasized the victim's story, and that shared how Katy came from a close-knit family with a history of looking out for each other.

"Like, the more I read about them, the more I was like, 'I just want to hang out with you guys,'" she said.

Urquhart pointed out that Katy was a high achiever in high school who enrolled at Clarkson to study business. The host noted how friends and family praised Katy as being one of the nicest individuals they knew, both to friends and strangers. Those who heard Katy's throaty laugh never forgot it.

Katy Hawelka, center, poses with friends at a Kappa Epsilon Phi high school sorority meeting in the early 1980s: Heather Conine, upper left; Martha Gualtieri, upper right; and Danielle Thomasmeyer, bottom left. (Hawelka family photo.)

"Now, Katy's friends and family only ever referred to her as Katy or Kate," Urquhart said, quoting from an early chapter in the book. "Her mom liked to call her, 'Never a bad day Kate.'"

"Stop," Kelley interjected softly. "So cute."

As the podcast turned to the morning of August 29, 1986, the hosts analyzed and debated the decision-making of the two Clarkson University security guards who had initially driven from the scene after mistaking the attack for a couple having consensual sex. Urquhart argued that their duty was to immediately intervene.

"You can't let people, like, be having sex outside," she said.

Kelley noted this was a different era when lots of institutions, including universities, weren't as strict with security.

"I also feel like this unfortunately happened in a time where we weren't looking into these things," she said.

The hosts agreed with Katy's family that she might still be alive if the two guards had intervened immediately. Not that Urquhart and Kelley placed all the blame on the men. Both were hired as night watchmen without police powers, and Clarkson didn't even provide them with two-way radios connected to the Potsdam Village Police.

"To play a bit of devil's advocate," Urquhart said, "because I truly don't think these security guards were properly trained at all for this shit, and that's on the university, to be quite honest.…They're not trained to observe that in the way that we're thinking about it, in that moment, right?…They're probably in the moment just like, 'Oh, God, I don't want to deal with this.'"

She pointed out that the guards, once they recognized what happened, rushed to call Potsdam police, who subsequently confronted McCarthy sprawled beneath an outdoors stairway alongside Walker Arena. When officers confronted him, he immediately concocted a story about how an unknown man in a black jacket attacked him from behind.

"He had blood on his shirt, and he was over dramatically whining and bitching about his back being hurt," Urquhart said. "Like they tried to pick him up, and he was like, 'No, no, no, my back. Ow-ee!' Like freaking out. …As they tried to ascertain who he was and what the fuck he was doing under the stairs near a woman who was battered beyond recognition, he kept asking, 'How's the girl?' And they found this strange. And it was also not coming off as sincere…because he knew what he did to her."

Urquhart concluded McCarthy's behavior made it evident he was "a lying sack of shit."

Initially, McCarthy denied he had any involvement in the attack, claiming he had never even seen the victim.

"He then asked if she was going to be all right, and said, quote, 'Somebody told me it was really bad.'" Urquhart paused. "Piece of shit."

As the first hour concluded, Urquhart said the second part would focus more on Katy and her family's fight to keep McCarthy from getting out of prison. Urquhart warned listeners "this does not have a happy ending. Katy does pass away. I just want you guys to know that."

The hosts then reminded listeners to consider signing the family's petition, and they posted a link to it with their podcast websites. Within the first week, the number of petition signatures ballooned by more than 3,000 to nearly 12,000, with many from other countries.

When the second part of "The Horrific Murder of Katy Hawelka" streamed on Friday, May 13, Urquhart and Kelley returned to the day of the attack, noting that McCarthy finally admitted to assaulting Katy only after a New York State Police investigator whom he knew since childhood encouraged him to tell the truth.

During a second interrogation, McCarthy admitted he had seen Katy walking back toward campus, escorted by a male friend. After the man left, McCarthy intercepted her behind the arena.

Urquhart expressed anger at how McCarthy, even in admitting his crime, kept making up details to minimize it, such as claiming Katy was bleeding even before he beat and kicked her. And when he got to the part about sexually assaulting Katy, McCarthy struggled to say what he did.

"This infuriates me," she said. "You can do it, but you're too chicken shit to relay it verbally. You fucking anal fissure. Like, are you kidding me?… Now this should tell you right here that he should be locked up forever, that he can't even say the words of what he did."

In his confession, McCarthy stated that he never raped Katy because he was unable to have an erection. Kelley wondered if McCarthy's deadly violence stemmed from drunken sexual frustration. Urquhart countered that McCarthy's confession revealed he had stalked Katy with the sole intent of forcing her into sex, killing her when she resisted.

"I think he's a demon, yeah," she said. "And I think he's a violent piece of shit. Oh, I think that. And I think he saw her, and he said, 'I'm going to rape her.' and 'I'm going to hurt her if she fights me, right?' And I think that was it. So, yeah. And I think she fought him back, and he hurt her, yeah."

As for McCarthy later blaming the attack on his use of drugs and alcohol, that is "an excuse," Urquhart said.

"Yeah, I think so," Kelley agreed.

"Now," Urquhart asked, "do you want to know what he said when they asked him, in 2009 at his parole hearing, how he came across Katy and what happened?"

"No," Kelley said, her hesitant tone suggesting she knew it was bad.

Urquhart read from the parole transcript where McCarthy claimed Katy asked him "if I wanted to participate in having sex, and I tried, and I couldn't, and she got mad and spit in my face, and that made me angry."

Urquhart paused briefly. When she resumed speaking, her voice was tight with her own anger.

"All the way 23 years after this happened, 23 years after this motherfucker went to jail and made up all kinds of shit, he is now still going to blame it on Katy," she said. "He is still going to change his story completely. This is him trying to get out. By the way, this is him trying to get parole. He makes up a totally different story."

Even after all these years in prison, it was clear McCarthy wasn't rehabilitated, Urquhart said.

Kelley agreed: "He's the kind of person who should never walk free. Ever."

The hosts pleaded with listeners to sign the petition.

Before the weekend was over, the number of signatures grew to about 19,000. Four days after that, it was 31,800.

Thousands more began to follow the family's **4KatyHawelka** Facebook page, where hundreds left comments that expressed opposition to McCarthy's parole, and many offered prayers for Katy's family.

On Facebook, Katy's family thanked "Morbid" for a "positive, empathetic view toward Katy" and the family's fight for justice. The family praised how the "two women hosts said they wished they had personally known Katy, and they thought her family was just something special as well."

In 2024, when asked about the podcast, 81-year-old Terry shared that she had listened to the entire two-hour program. Although phrases like "sack of shit" and "anal fissure" weren't part of her own vocabulary, she noted that she wasn't bothered in the slightest by their use to describe her daughter's killer.

"No, not at all," she said, her expression steely. "Actually, I thought it was done well."

As the 2023 parole hearing date drew nearer, Katy's family discovered through a DOCCS website directory that McCarthy had been transferred to Groveland Correctional Facility in western New York. The timing of the move, just weeks before the scheduled April hearing, raised suspicions. Similar transfers in the past had occurred after McCarthy received disciplinary tickets, which often led to hearing delays while he appealed.

Betsy McInerney contacted the Office of Victim Assistance in Albany for clarification. A staff member assured her that McCarthy's hearing was still scheduled for the last week of April but provided no explanation for the transfer or word of any disciplinary infractions.

On April 1, the family posted the following message on its Facebook page:

> We learned by chance yesterday, March 31st that the inmate has been transferred to a similar medium security facility in Livingston County called Groveland. Typically, inmates are transferred if there is an infraction. He had been housed at the Cayuga facility for the past 6 years, so this is unsettling. NO information is being shared with our family. He is tentatively scheduled to appear the week of April 24, 2023. Best case scenario for us is that he got into some trouble that would almost guarantee a denial of parole. There is also a possibility that his parole hearing would be postponed until the infraction issue is resolved.
>
> Office of Victims Assistance can only confirm minimal vague details which is beyond frustrating! We have no choice but to wait for updates the week of May 1st. Unacceptable that we are kept in the dark and for that reason we ask that you continue to support our efforts to get the appearance extended to a maximum of 60 months following a denial of parole.
>
> Heartbreaking that this convicted murderer still has a right to privacy. Please keep the faith that when this monster appears before the parole commissioners, he is DENIED parole.

Shortly afterward, DOCCS updated its website to show McCarthy's parole hearing had been rescheduled for June.

On May 3, an employee at the Office of Victim Assistance informed Katy's brother that McCarthy had been transferred on March 27 due to another disciplinary ticket, with the hearing now expected as late as July. No details about the alleged offense were provided.

In a group email to the family, Joe Hawelka Jr. described the news as "good," saying it was more evidence that McCarthy could not be trusted to stay out of trouble.

Betsy filed a Freedom of Information request seeking details about the incident. DOCCS responded with a one-page report that redacted most of the wording. The report confirmed, however, that McCarthy received a mid-level Tier 2 ticket at 10 a.m. on March 27 for violating Rule 180.11, related to facility correspondence procedures. A hearing on April 25 resulted in McCarthy receiving "counsel," essentially a verbal warning.

The parole board eventually scheduled McCarthy's eighth parole hearing for June 27.

Even then, behind the scenes, McCarthy pushed for another delay. The inmate who was so proud of his cleaning skills wanted more time to sanitize his parole file before his next meeting with commissioners.

Chapter 7

McCarthy's 2023 Parole Hearing

BRIAN McCarthy stared at his latest COMPAS scores, frustration boiling. To him, the April 2023 screening didn't just exaggerate his risk—some information in it was flat-out wrong. If left uncorrected, he clearly feared, COMPAS would no longer be the tool that helped make his case that he was not a felony risk if granted parole.

As his parole hearing date neared, McCarthy ramped up the pressure on Groveland Correctional Facility staff, demanding they revise the scores, according to a transcript of the hearing. (The heavily redacted transcript didn't disclose McCarthy's latest COMPAS scores, but it was clear this time his concerns went beyond his risk number for substance abuse.)

By early June, McCarthy was also complaining about access to the prison's Resource Center, where inmates attend educational and vocational programs for reintegration into the community. He also voiced confusion about receiving multiple notices with conflicting dates for his hearing.

Finally, on June 9, Senior Offender Rehabilitation Coordinator Amy Hornberger notified McCarthy by letter to stop trying to "argue your position and be uncooperative at your interviews" with prison staff. The letter read, in part:

> You met with ORC Corrine on June 9th, 2023, at 8:30 a.m. and made accusations that you have submitted several written correspondences to participate and attend the Resource Center. I have consulted with both coordinators of the program and found this information to be incorrect. Both coordinators report receiving no written correspondence from you.

> Additionally, you have expressed on June 8th, 2023, and June 9th, 2023, your dissatisfaction with your COMPAS scores. You have received directions from ORC and myself that you can discuss this with the Commissioners at your June 23rd reappearance board. You have continued to argue your position and have been uncooperative at the interviews. This will serve as your last reminder that all questions regarding COMPAS risk scores will be addressed at your upcoming Parole Board.
>
> Additionally, you reported to ORC Corrine on June 9th, 2023, that your April '23 Parole Board was postponed due to a discrepancy on your COMPAS. This is incorrect information. The transcripts are clear that a request to postpone your board was due to submit an updated parole packet.

After receiving this warning, McCarthy decided he couldn't wait until his hearing to complain to the parole board. He outlined his concerns in a letter dated June 12 and addressed it to "Parole Board Commissioners," including with it a copy of Hornberger's letter.

On the afternoon of Tuesday, June 27, as McCarthy's eighth parole hearing got underway, he was still fighting to get his scores changed. One of Commissioner Chanwoo Lee's first questions hinted at McCarthy's reluctance to attend the hearing.

"So, you joined us for your reappearance, correct, sir?" she asked via a video link from the parole office in Buffalo, where she was accompanied by commissioners Marc Coppola and Joseph Crangle.

"I did," McCarthy said.

"Are you ready to go, sir?"

"Well," McCarthy said, "there's a couple things that I would like to bring up before I get into the—"

Lee interrupted. "Okay. Is it about your COMPAS, sir? Is it about your COMPAS?"

"It is."

Lee made a brief, redacted comment before continuing. "Is that the only thing that you want to talk about, sir?"

New York State Parole Board commissioners, from left, Chanwoo Lee, Joseph Crangle and Marc Coppola. (Department of Corrections and Community Supervision photo.)

"No. There's other issues."

Lee asked, "What other issues, sir?" She noted that McCarthy had since April to resolve any with DOCCS staff.

"I am not sure. I am still trying to figure that out," he said hesitantly.

"Okay. What's your issue, sir? Come on."

His response, partially redacted, made it clear he was still focused on his COMPAS scores.

"Well, I have a couple numbers off. This one is off. The one I have is a little bit off," McCarthy said, with the transcript redacting the specific scores.

"All right. Sir, you know what?" Lee said. "I will make a notation of your objection, sir. This (COMPAS report) is only a tool. It is not a controlling factor, sir. This is a tool that we use as part of our decision-making process, sir."

Lee previously worked in criminal defense for a legal aid society in New York City. This was the first hearing with McCarthy for both Lee and Crangle, a former probation officer. However, this was the fourth time Coppola served on McCarthy's parole panel.

After addressing McCarthy's concerns about COMPAS, Lee asked, "Anything else?"

McCarthy complained he received notices on May 11, then May 17 and finally on June 8 about dates of his hearing. "It went from 60 days to 90 days and back to 60 days, and it confused me because I wasn't able to prepare."

That mattered, he said finally, because "I am trying to challenge the book you have in your possession written against me."

"What book are you talking about? What book are you referring to?" Lee asked.

"There was a novel," he said.

Lee held up a copy of "A Stranger Killed Katy," possibly one that Betsy McInerney had submitted to the parole board with her impact statement.

"I am talking about that," McCarthy said, referring to the book. "I am asking for a postponement because I am looking to have that extracted from my file."

The transcript did not clarify who had placed the book in McCarthy's file. If it came from Betsy, McCarthy shouldn't have seen it—or even known it was there—since submissions with family impact statements are considered confidential under parole Directive 2014.

"Sir, when did you find out that there was a book in the file, sir?" Lee asked.

"When I reviewed my parole file."

"When was that, sir?"

"I want to say that it was June 8th, I believe," McCarthy said.

Lee pointed out that inmates have strict rules they must follow when seeking a delay of a parole hearing.

"Sir, you have 10 days to request a postponement. You have 10 days. You just said you were aware of this book June 6th, I believe you said—"

"Right. That's why I asked you about the confusion."

"Excuse me, sir. I am talking. We can't talk at the same time," Lee said.

"Okay," McCarthy said.

"Did you write a letter to DOCCS asking for a postponement? You had enough time. Today is June 27th and," she began, then paused abruptly. "You know what? Listen, you have been around the block, so to speak, with this board, right? You know that you are entitled to a postponement."

McCarthy claimed he tried, referring to the June 12 correspondence he sent to the parole board with a copy of Hornberger's letter.

Lee pulled out a copy. She noted how his letter mentioned COMPAS, but there was nothing in there about a book.

"Look at your letter, sir. Do you say anything about a book being removed from your parole packet, sir?" she asked.

"No," McCarthy admitted, complaining that changes in his hearing date left him "confused" and unable to properly prepare.

"I was given three notices," he said, "so I didn't know which one to refer to, and then I reviewed my file, and I found out that there were issues in my file that I needed to have access to."

Lee noted that McCarthy's attorney, Cheryl L. Kates, had submitted his parole plan on June 7 without requesting a postponement.

At this point, Lee went off the record. The hearing was now several minutes old, with still no discussion of McCarthy's suitability for parole.

When she went back on the record, Lee said she would make sure the record noted McCarthy's objection to the book. But its appearance in the parole file, Lee said, was a "legal matter that is outside the purview of this board, okay?"

McCarthy still wasn't satisfied.

"So, I am not being granted a postponement until I can review legal evidence to have that removed?" McCarthy asked.

Lee repeated that McCarthy's objections to the book were not grounds to further delay the hearing.

"That's an outside legal issue, sir. It may take years for you to challenge that to have it removed from the board packet. That's something that you have to deal with, all right, sir? I will make a notation of your objection over that book in your file, all right?"

"So, is that a denial?" McCarthy asked. "I am being denied a postponement based on the three things that I brought up: the COMPAS, the notification of—"

Lee interrupted, trying to move the hearing along, but McCarthy continued pressing for a postponement.

Finally, Commissioner Crangle spoke up, reminding McCarthy he had the option of participating in the hearing or not.

"Sir, the bottom line is, we are going to go forward," Crangle said. "If you want to sit there and not answer any questions regarding your future in terms of your plans, the offense, that's on you. But we are going forward.

We already spent 15 minutes discussing things, and Commissioner Lee has been very specific. We have everything. We are going forward."

McCarthy decided to stay, but he wasn't happy.

"I just want to make sure this is on the record that I am asking for a postponement, and we are going on with this hearing. Is that what you are telling me?" McCarthy asked.

"Yes," Lee said.

"Okay."

"Yes. Your objection is noted, sir."

And with that, Lee turned to the events of August 29, 1986, when McCarthy beat, sexually assaulted, and fatally strangled Katy.

Lee read aloud the original criminal complaint by Potsdam Village Police, which alleged that McCarthy engaged in "sexual intercourse with a female victim by forcible compulsion and without the victim's consent." The police based these allegations on witness statements, "physical evidence collected and preserved from the bodies of the subject and the victim," and McCarthy's own admissions, Lee said.

"So, tell me, what happened, sir? What's going on here?" Lee asked. "Who's the victim?"

"It was an acquaintance," McCarthy said, sticking with his claim to know Katy prior to the attack. "I was introduced to her at a college campus."

"How did you meet her?"

"Through people on the campus."

"And you said she was [redacted] years old?"

"Yes."

"Were you attending college at that school?"

"No, I was not."

"What were you doing?" Lee asked.

"I lived in that town," he said.

"I see. Were you working or going to school or what?"

"Yes. I was working."

Lee asked for names of students he knew at Clarkson. McCarthy offered a first name, which was blacked out in the transcript.

"Last name?" she asked.

"It's been a long time," he said.

"All right."

McCarthy offered another first name.

"Last name?"

"[Redacted] I believe her name was."

"What were they studying?"

"I don't know," he said.

"What year were they? Were they freshman, sophomore, junior?"

"I want to say they were juniors."

Lee returned to McCarthy's claim he knew Katy prior to the morning he attacked her.

"Okay. And when was the first time you met the victim, sir?"

"Probably the year before."

"1985?"

"Yes. I believe so."

"What month?"

"I am not even sure."

"Summer? Fall? Give me an estimate. Come on," Lee said.

"It would probably be the fall because it was—I think it was chilly. I am not sure," McCarthy said.

"Okay. And under what circumstance did you meet her, where?" Lee asked.

"Through college campus personnel that were there, friends that I knew that were at the college campus in the dorms," he said vaguely.

Lee pressed harder, aiming to get a clear answer, while McCarthy parried with brief, guarded responses, sidestepping specifics.

"So," Lee asked, "you met her in a dorm, or you met her in the personnel office? Where did you meet her? I am asking you *where*."

"In the dorm."

"Dorm. Okay. And how many times did you see her prior to this day, sir?"

"Say that again," McCarthy said.

"How many times did you encounter the victim prior to this rape and murder?"

"I don't know. Two or three maybe."

"Where did you meet her?" Lee asked again.

This time, McCarthy's answer was even less specific.

"In the campus," he said.

"Just campus?"

"No. There was a hockey game. We went to a hockey game one night. I ended up getting some tickets."

"Which hockey game?" Lee asked.

"Clarkson University."

"Do you know the date or month?"

"No, I do not."

"And you said you saw her twice, right?"

"Yes. Possibly twice, maybe three times."

"But you weren't friends, right?"

"No. We were just introduced to each other."

Lee moved on to the morning of the attack.

"So, what were you doing on the campus at 3:30 in the morning on August 29th, 1986?"

"We were with some friends."

"When you say 'we,' who are you talking about? I wasn't there," Lee said.

"People that lived in the town," McCarthy said.

"Okay. Who would that be, sir?"

"I have no idea who they are," he said brusquely. "Last names. First names. Introducing each other. Having an evening out."

Lee wanted to know what McCarthy and his acquaintances were doing on campus at that early hour.

"Going to the dorms," McCarthy said.

"At 3:30 in the morning?"

"It's college."

"Which dorm were you going to exactly?"

"I don't remember the names of the dorms, but it was across the street from the hockey arena."

"And who were the people that you were visiting?" Lee asked.

"I can't remember that," McCarthy said. "That was almost 37 years old."

"Okay. You said you were there with somebody else from the town. Who are those people, sir?" Lee asked.

He answered, "People that were in the bar drinking, people that were in the bar playing pool, people that were in the bar playing in the band."

She was pressing for the kinds of verifiable details that would give his story some credibility. However, McCarthy stopped short of saying which bar, or which people he met playing pool, or which musicians were performing in the band, or which people walked toward Clarkson with him that morning.

"Okay," Lee said. "They went with you to campus at 3:30 in the morning with the intent to go to the dorm to visit somebody?"

"Yes."

Lee paused to note she had read McCarthy's presentencing report from 1987, and what he was saying now didn't match that summary.

"There seems to be a little bit of a different statement along the way, put it that way," Lee said.

McCarthy had no response to that, so Lee continued pressing for details on what he was doing at the university at that time of day.

"So, how are you going to get access to the dorm? Isn't it locked down at 3:30 in the morning?" she asked.

"No. You just walk through the campus," he said. Looking back, there was some truth to this claim. Although Clarkson University in the 1980s required dorms to be locked at night, residents often propped doors open for friends or for students returning late from downtown.

"Okay. But this was a Clarkson University property, right, sir?"

"Yes."

Lee wanted to know if McCarthy had consent from anyone to be on campus at 3:30 in the morning.

"I don't think you need consent," he said. "You just go to the campus and visit your friends."

Lee pointed out to McCarthy that he neither went to school at Clarkson nor worked there.

"No. I am a local, though," he said.

"Okay," she said. "But a local doesn't have a right to be there if you don't go to that school, right? This is a private university, correct, sir?"

"It is."

"So, you were there without the consent of the property owner, the university. Would that be fair to say, sir?"

"I don't know what the rights are of the campus. I don't know if you are allowed to go on there."

"Okay. But we agreed this is a private university, correct, sir?" she asked.

"It is a private university," McCarthy conceded.

"All right."

As Lee shifted the discussion to the attack on Katy, the commissioner quickly made it clear that she was frustrated with McCarthy's evasive answers and his frequent claims of memory loss.

"How did you encounter the victim, sir?"

"We had agreed that we were going to have casual sex, and I couldn't perform and when she spit in my face, it was a knee-jerk reaction—"

Lee interrupted. "Okay. How did you meet her?"

"And I went to protect myself," McCarthy said, finishing his answer.

For the third time, Lee asked her question.

"How did you meet her, sir?"

"Walking back to the campus," McCarthy said finally.

"And what about the people you were with, where were they?" Lee asked.

"They were in their own little world. They were doing their thing," McCarthy said.

"Okay. Were they with you when you ran into the victim?"

"No."

Lee asked how he first encountered Katy. "Who saw who first, you or her? she asked.

"I don't remember," McCarthy replied.

"Who initiated the conversation between you and her?"

"I think she did."

Lee wanted to know if Katy said, "I want to have sex with you. Let's do a one-night quickie." The commissioner's choice of words teetered on mockery, but McCarthy seemed not to notice.

"Yeah," he said of Lee's description, adding that Katy told him, "I remember you. You are a good-looking guy. I saw you on campus," and "we kind of agreed."

"Okay. Really?" Lee asked.

"Yeah."

"Okay. And then what happened?"

"I was drinking, and I was inebriated, and I couldn't perform, and she got disgusted, got mad and spit in my face," he said. "And I didn't realize that she was spitting in my face, and I went to protect myself, and I ended up hitting her."

"All right," Lee asked. "How did you hit her?"

"With an open hand," McCarthy said.

"Where did you hit her? What part of her body did you hit her?"

"I hit her on the head. I didn't do it with intention to hurt her. I did it with intention because it's a knee-jerk reaction.…It surprised me so I didn't intend to do it with malice, but obviously I did."

It was clear McCarthy had wanted the parole board to disregard the autopsy report showing that Katy suffered "numerous external body injuries." Many were classic defensive wounds, including a compound fracture to Katy's right index finger. The autopsy found bruises on her forearms, two black eyes, swelling and bleeding of the nose, and bruising to Katy's face, neck, and shoulders.

Lee asked if Katy fell after he struck her.

"Yes. She fell."

"And then what? You tried to have sex with her?"

"No. Because I couldn't perform," he said.

"Was she intoxicated?"

"Absolutely."

"Okay. The record indicated that she was intoxicated, and she was unconscious, right?"

"Yes."

"So how—"

McCarthy interrupted Lee. Maybe he believed she was about to ask how come he tried to have sex with Katy while she was unconscious.

"Wait a minute," he said. "Was she unconscious? I don't know about that."

"When you found her, was she conscious or not conscious?"

"She was conscious."

Lee asked if he took her clothes off.

"*She* started to," he answered.

"She took her clothes off in the middle of the night at 3:30 in the morning to have one quickie on the campus?" Lee asked.

"She started to."

"Okay. While you were trying to do that, did anybody come by and see you on top of her?"

"Oh, I don't know. You will have to ask them."

McCarthy wasn't going to confirm the statements of the two security guards who saw him with his pants down, engaged in what they mistakenly believed was consensual intercourse.

Lee asked McCarthy to describe how he assaulted Katy.

"I hit her."

"How?"

"With my hand. I just explained that."

"How many times?"

"Once," he said.

If true, why did the autopsy find Katy died from strangulation? Lee asked.

"I don't—you would have to read the autopsy to figure that out, because I didn't do that," McCarthy said. "I admitted that I assaulted, and I attempted to rape this woman, and it was my mistake because I was inebriated, and I couldn't perform that sexual request. And being that I was frustrated—I didn't have the opportunity to explain myself: She had someone else's ID, and they asked me when they showed me the ID if I knew her, and they showed me an ID—"

Lee cut him off. McCarthy had veered back to his confusing claim from 2021 that the police wrongly believed he denied knowing Katy in 1986 because they showed him her cousin's ID card.

"I need you to slow down, sir," Lee said. "You are getting way off track. Who asked you if you knew her? You are going way ahead of the game, sir."

"Oh, okay. I thought you wanted to hear what happened. That's what happened," McCarthy said.

"Well, I am going to ask you next what happened, sir."

"Okay."

"You hit her and assaulted her, then what? How did you end up getting arrested?" Lee asked.

"Yes. I got hit in the back of the head."

"By her?"

"I don't know by who," McCarthy said, changing his story from the 2021 parole hearing where he explicitly stated Katy never hit him. "They found me face-down on the ground."

"Were you near her, next to her?" Lee asked.

"I think so. I am not sure," McCarthy said.

Lee asked McCarthy what happened next.

"I don't know. The next thing I knew I woke up in the ambulance." He was wearing a neck brace, McCarthy said, but he couldn't remember if there was blood on his shirt or boots because "they took all my clothes."

"Did you see the victim being taken away from the location, sir?"

"No. I was on the ground, face down," he said.

"Okay. At some point you learned that she died, right?"

"Yes," McCarthy said. "Three days later."

"And then that's when the (assault) charge was upgraded to murder in the second, correct, sir?"

"It is," he said.

With that, Lee turned to McCarthy's history of arrests and convictions, both in New York and Virginia.

"How many times have you been arrested in your life, sir, all together just in New York State?"

"I don't know. I know there has been a few," McCarthy said.

"What's a few? Give me a number. I don't know. You must know," Lee said.

"Eight or nine, probably."

"It says you have been arrested nine times, four convictions, four felonies, one violent felony," Lee said, reading from McCarthy's file. "I am assuming including this one, okay? That's what your rap sheet says."

It was unclear which record Lee was viewing, because other documents showed at least 12 arrests in New York, not including ones when he was a youthful offender. He also had at least four more in Virginia.

The transcript redacted another exchange before the commissioner began listing specific arrests. There were so many, Lee had trouble keeping them straight.

"July 9th, 1984, possession of stolen property," Lee read aloud. "Now, was this in Virginia, possession of stolen property, conditional discharge, or was it in New York?"

"I don't know. I don't have my record in front of me," McCarthy said.

"Okay. July 12th (1984) you were rearrested for criminal possession in the second (degree with a) conditional discharge. You were (also) arrested in Virginia for statutory burglary and grand larceny, (with) supervised indefinite probation."

McCarthy tried to point out something. "All of those are convictions with—"

"And I am not finished, sir," Lee said, cutting him off.

"January 13th, 1985, you were arrested for unauthorized use of a motor vehicle in Richmond City, Virginia. You got two years prison, served 11 months…and I believe you were on parole for that case when you committed the instant offense, correct, sir?"

"I believe you are right," McCarthy conceded.

Lee wasn't done. She noted McCarthy returned to New York, where on March 4, 1986, he was arrested for petit larceny, resulting in 60 days in jail.

"This is a lot of arrests," she said.

"All of those are convictions or just arrests?" McCarthy asked.

"Fourteen arrests altogether. But you do have convictions in New York and Virginia, correct, sir?"

"I believe so, yes."

"You should know," Lee said. "You are the one that got arrested, right?"

She continued without waiting for an answer. She appeared intent on making a point that Katy was murdered by a career criminal who didn't stop violating the law even when on parole.

"Looking at your record, right?" Lee said. "I mean, that behavior escalated to this, right? This violent heinous crime, right? It caused the loss of a life, right?"

"Right."

"So why do you think that is the case, sir?" she asked.

McCarthy's initial response was redacted, but it was clear he had repeated his claim that he had been sexually molested as a teen.

"And how I escalated from petit larceny and larcenous behavior to second-degree murder and attempted rape was because of the aggravation. I took that out, and I didn't have the right to do that, nor did I have the avenue to do that," McCarthy said.

Lee indicated that she found nothing in the record showing that McCarthy mentioned the molestation before he applied for parole.

"Well, you don't feel too comfortable telling people about that," McCarthy said.

"When was the first time you raised that issue, when you came out?"

"When I came out? Came out with what?" McCarthy asked.

"I am asking you what year, at what point?" Lee said.

"I don't remember what year it was."

Lee reframed her question.

"Was it during the parole board, after the initial interview, before the parole interview or what?"

"I am not even sure."

Lee moved on, but the implication was clear: McCarthy's claim of being a victim of child abuse would carry more weight if he revealed it long before he used it before the parole board as an excuse for his crimes.

Commissioner Crangle spoke up again. He still had questions about McCarthy's account of encountering Katy.

"When you were outside with her, you both were under the influence of alcohol, correct?" he asked.

"Yes. She was underage, and I was drinking, yes."

Crangle asked McCarthy if he was saying Katy struck him, and then he retaliated by hitting her.

"No. I didn't say she hit me," McCarthy said. "She spit in my face....And she laughed at me and humiliated me. But at the same time if someone is in your proximity and they spit in your face and it surprises you, your instant knee-jerk reaction is to bring your hand up to protect yourself."

McCarthy maintained that he didn't mean to hurt Katy.

"I ended up hitting her in her face. It wasn't intentional. It was a complete mistake. Did I intend to hit this girl? Absolutely not, Mr. Crangle. I owned up to what I did. I pled guilty to second-degree murder and attempted rape."

"Right," Crangle said.

"There is no DNA, and I know what I did. I know what I did," McCarthy said, attempting to steer the conversation to his other new claim from 2021.

Crangle wasn't allowing the diversion.

"So, after you reacted—when you reacted from her spitting in your face, you hit her, you stated, right? Due to your—"

McCarthy interrupted. "Yes. The knee-jerk reaction, yes….It wasn't out of aggression. Let me put it that way. It wasn't where I was doing it on purpose to knock her down because she spit in my face, and when someone does that and it surprises you, your reaction is to protect yourself."

"Okay."

"And I didn't realize she was that close. So, when I brought my hand up to swing at her and push her away, it wasn't done intentionally."

Crangle asked how McCarthy ended up being unconscious before the police arrived.

"I got hit."

"Okay. And you don't know who hit you?"

"I have no idea who hit me."

"Well, what was she doing?" Crangle asked. "After you hit her, was she just passed out?"

"How am I supposed to know if I am face down and someone hit me from behind? How am I supposed to know what's going on?" McCarthy said.

"Right after you hit her, what did you do? The next thing you know, you are waking up?"

"I was waking up on the ground. I was being put in the ambulance, I believe."

"That's the last thing—so really the last thing you remember is you hitting her?" Crangle asked.

"Yes."

"And then all a sudden, before you know it, you are in the ambulance and questions are being asked?"

"And they are accusing me of something, and I was like, 'I don't think you're accusing me of the right stuff.' I mean, there's no DNA. I asked him, I said, 'Why am I being accused of rape? I didn't rape this girl,' and that's why I pled guilty to attempted rape. If that's the scenario that they want to go with, I can understand that, Mr. Crangle. But at the same time, I keep trying to emphasize that when I hit this girl, it was not my intent to do harm."

McCarthy continued, "We had agreed upon each other's request, whether we were on an alcohol binge, you know, or if it was one of those things where you just don't really think about it. I would assume that you have had a few drinks before, and you don't think too clearly."

Crangle, passing up a chance to discuss his own alcohol use, asked McCarthy to clarify how much time elapsed between his claim that he hit Katy once and getting struck himself.

"So, it was pretty immediate?"

"I am not sure."

"No," Crangle said. "I just mean, to you it was immediate because you don't remember anything after hitting her because you were all a sudden woken up by the authorities, right?"

"I don't know who woke me up. I have no idea who woke me up."

Lee picked up on Crangle's line of questioning, "So, when you were arrested, what did you tell the police?" she asked. She perhaps hoped McCarthy would at least concede his current story differed from his confession in 1986.

Instead, he said, "I don't remember."

"You don't remember," Lee said flatly. "Did you—"

McCarthy interrupted. "No, I do not remember."

"Did you give a written statement? Did you confess to the cop?"

"I don't remember what I said to them."

In 1986, Potsdam police referred to McCarthy after his arrest as an unemployed drifter who had been living in a friend's cabin in Madrid, a small town about 10 miles from Potsdam.

Lee wanted to hear from McCarthy if he was working at the time of Katy's murder.

"I believe I was doing carpentry work," McCarthy said, adding that he had helped a friend build a house. "His name was [redacted]. He's dead."

Lee noted McCarthy's parole application included a resume with numerous jobs in the early to mid-1980s, including 18 months he claimed he spent at a Florida mirror imaging detail company, and eight months "loading and unloading" for another employer.

Lee then produced McCarthy's Virginia parole report from 1985 where McCarthy listed a different group of jobs for much shorter periods.

The current parole resume "seems to be a little bit of an embellishment, is that correct?" Lee asked.

McCarthy said he had to rely on memory for his resume because his prison property was stolen, "so I don't have all the records that I fought for."

"I see," she said.

"And I tried to get the documents, but I can't refer to them if I tried to get them. Do you understand what I mean?"

"Okay. So do you think—"

McCarthy interrupted again. "It's kind of hard to remember when you are trying to get all the information to present to the parole board—" he said.

"So, do you think your memory—"

McCarthy complained, "You are not even letting me finish."

"Do you think your memory is fresher now than it was back in the 1980s?" Lee asked.

"I have a hard time remembering what I ate for breakfast this morning," he replied.

"Okay," Lee said finally. "Sir, we will just move on, sir."

Lee noted for the record that McCarthy's attorney had provided the board with a parole packet that included his personal statement, a COMPAS risk assessment, and certificates of completion of numerous prison programs.

McCarthy's parole application also mentioned that he had written a letter to Katy's family and sent it to the Office of Victim Assistance's "Apology

Letter Bank." The repository allows victims and their families to choose whether to read the messages without having direct contact with an inmate.

McCarthy also in 2021 sent to the repository a copy of his "personal statement" in which he complained to the parole board that "my feelings are not adequately being portrayed" at hearings and that often "my answers are being misconstrued." He also repeated that he knew Katy "in passing," that she "did not deserve to die or suffer the pain I inflicted on her," and that he had Masses said several times in her memory.

Lee expressed puzzlement over the tone and content of McCarthy's similar personal statement to the parole board in 2023.

"I mean, you talk about, you know, the damage you created in the victim's life, but you don't really talk about your crime. You don't talk about what you did to her, which was interesting," Lee said. "So, I looked at your other personal statements, and you talk about your crime. But again, you don't go into detail about what you did, and I thought that was kind of interesting because I get many, many personal statements, and they talk about what they did."

McCarthy asked Lee how many parole plans that she had in front of her.

Each of his since 2009, she said, before a further exchange that was mostly redacted in the transcript.

Lee turned to McCarthy's submissions of psychological reports by Peter P. "Maximilian" Buonocore, the Newark, New Jersey, licensed professional counselor and ordained priest who concluded McCarthy was not at risk for reoffending. The transcript redacted Buonocore's name, but it was clear from the discussion that Lee was referring to him.

"Do you know where he went to school?"

While McCarthy dug through some kind of record to come up with an answer, Lee asked how many times the two met after his initial assessment in 2011.

"Five, six, ten, twelve. More than that maybe."

"And how did you end up contacting him? Did he contact you or did you reach out to him?"

"Through my fiancée. He's a friend of mine."

Lee asked, "He's a friend of yours?" leaving it unclear whether she was merely confirming what McCarthy said, or perhaps subtly questioning the objectivity of Buonocore's report.

"Yes," McCarthy said.

"Are you the first person he assessed who was incarcerated for murder?" Lee asked.

"I have no idea what that means. I have no idea what you are even asking me," McCarthy said.

It was clear that Lee wanted to know about Buonocore's experience in evaluating convicted murderers, but she decided to drop the matter.

"Well, I read his report, and I will take it into consideration, okay?" Lee said.

A few minutes later, McCarthy announced that Buonocore had three PhDs.

"All right," Lee said. "Do you know where he went to school? That's what I am asking you. I know you said he's—"

McCarthy cut her off to express frustration at questions about Buonocore's background.

"I am trying to give you the best answer," he said, "but you are trying to make it confrontational. I am just trying to help you understand."

"No, sir, you are the one who is—"

"See, Ms. Lee, please, I am trying to be cordial. I am trying to answer your questions. You are not giving me a chance."

"Sir, I am asking you a question. You are talking over me, sir. You are the one who is getting a little bit upset and aggravated."

"No. I am not getting upset," McCarthy said. "Absolutely not. If I was getting upset, I would get up and leave. I am trying to help you understand because you are not giving me an opportunity to express myself."

"All right. I asked you whether you knew the educational background of (Buonocore). You said you didn't know. That's fine. We will just move on, sir."

Contacted in 2024, Buonocore stated he had a bachelor's degree in engineering from Catholic University of America, and a master's degree in counseling psychology and one in theology, both from Seton Hall University. His credentials also were listed at the website for St. Benedict's Prep School, operated by the Newark Abbey. Buonocore didn't list any PhDs.

Lee wanted to know about McCarthy's fiancée, noting she had provided a letter of support for him.

"And you are not married to her, correct?" Lee asked.

"No. We are engaged," McCarthy said.

Parole boards are often skeptical of such relationships, as it's not uncommon for inmates to identify a female friend as a fiancée to show a support system waiting upon release, which can bolster their case for parole.

Lee asked, "When was the last time you spoke to your fiancée?"

"I want to say yesterday," McCarthy said.

"And how long has she been your fiancée?"

"Since 2003."

"How did you meet her?"

"We went to the same high school," McCarthy said.

"What year did she graduate?"

"I am not sure."

Lee was puzzled. McCarthy's prior answer had left the impression he met the woman while attending high school together.

"All right. I thought she was older than you," Lee said.

"She is older than me."

"By how many years, sir?"

"13."

"So, she could not be in the same school if she was…(13) years older than you, right? You could not—"

"My grandmother taught her, so I think we did go to the same school."

"But you didn't go to school at the same time."

"I didn't say that" she did, McCarthy said.

"Okay," Lee said. "Well, you said—okay. I didn't put words into your mouth, all right?"

"No, you did not. I said we went to the same school."

"All right. Same school," Lee acknowledged. "And how did you meet her? That's what I'm asking. Thirteen years' difference—I mean, most people would say they don't know anyone who went to school 13 years ago. You know what I'm saying?"

"No, I don't," McCarthy replied.

Lee took a moment to explain that a fiancée wasn't usually defined as family, which may explain "why you are highly probable…"

The transcript blacked out the rest of her comment. But her "highly probable" remark was a clue that perhaps the latest COMPAS didn't give McCarthy the positive score for family support that it had in the past.

"So how did you meet her then?" Lee asked.

"Interactions through social people involved in my family."

"Okay," Lee said. "And who would that be, your immediate family?"

"Yes."

"Who would that be, your mother, father, siblings?"

"Well, my mother is dead so—"

"I am sorry to hear that."

"Thank you," McCarthy said, adding that his mother was "kind of the connecting bridge that I had with my family. But they moved on, and they don't really have interaction with me."

Lee asked about McCarthy's father.

"He's alive. He retired," McCarthy said.

"When was the last time you had contact with your father?"

"It's been quite a few years."

"Okay. What about your siblings, when was the last time you had contact with them?

"I spoke to two of my brothers not too long ago. Within the last couple of years," McCarthy said without explaining how that squared with his earlier claim that his family didn't really have any interaction with him.

"Okay. But they have not come to visit you probably, right?"

"Yes, they have."

"When?"

"I want to say the year was 2005 maybe. There was a more recent one, too," he said.

Commissioner Crangle wanted to know more about McCarthy's life in prison.

"Sir, how are you spending your day at Groveland? What's your schedule like?" he asked.

"I go to the law library. I try to research. I try to stay away from the drugs. I don't do drugs. I have learned my lesson. Mr. Crangle, I know I had a bad crime," McCarthy said, pivoting away from discussing prison life to offer another pitch as to why he deserved parole. "I tried everything in my power to try to redeem—"

"Hold on," Crangle said.

"Please hear me out," McCarthy said.

The commissioner said he wasn't done asking about McCarthy's prison schedule, a key component in the board's evaluation.

"I want to finish what I wanted to go through with you," Crangle said firmly.

"Before you do that, I want an opportunity because you've never met me before," McCarthy insisted.

"Sir," Crangle said, "every time I am trying to talk to you, you are talking over me. Just give me a minute. I have been doing this for 15 years."

"Okay. I know. I read your bio. I know who you are," McCarthy said.

"Oh, there's a file on me?" Crangle asked.

"Yeah, there is."

If McCarthy intended for his remarks to turn the tables on the commissioners, Crangle wasn't playing that game. He responded with nothing more than a lighthearted remark.

"Really? Can I get a copy? Wait. Am I entitled to a copy?" Crangle asked.

"And Coppola, too."

"Oh, and Coppola. Really?"

"Yeah. Mr. Coppola," McCarthy said.

Crangle steered the conversation back to his original line of questioning.

"Anyhow, so you go to the law library. What else do you do?"

"I work out. I stay pretty healthy," McCarthy said.

"How do you keep the time rolling, is my point, in a healthy way?"

"I read a lot. I am pretty adamant about working out. You know, I stay pretty healthy."

Crangle wanted to know if McCarthy helped other prisoners in the law library.

"I do sometimes. It depends. There are certain avenues that I am good at," McCarthy said.

On the other hand, he said, if an inmate asked about the Time Allowance Committee, "I don't have a clue," referring to prison panels that recommend good-behavior early release for eligible inmates. McCarthy suggested he never learned about that because he was serving a life sentence that made him ineligible.

"I try to help when I can certain guys," McCarthy said, "and I don't know what else to say. But if I can give it back, I would give it back in a minute, and that's my pay it forward to people that come in the system."

Without waiting for another question, McCarthy suggested the commissioners already had their minds made up about him.

"I know I am probably going to get denied parole. I am not a fool. I am trying the best I can after almost 37 years," he said. "And Commissioner Lee, she challenged me. She hit me with some pretty hard stuff to make me think about stuff that I haven't thought about in a long time. Was I an idiot? Absolutely. But I am trying to do the best I can. I don't get in trouble. I don't use drugs. I try to help when I can, and I try to be as truthful as I can."

Rather than correct McCarthy's suggestion the panel had already made up its mind to deny him parole again, Crangle turned to McCarthy's teen years.

"Like back then when you were growing up and you got in trouble, why was it that you were—"

McCarthy interrupted with comments that, although redacted, appeared to refer again to being molested.

"And that caused you to do what?" Crangle asked.

"Rebel."

Crangle wanted to know how.

"Getting in trouble, being bad, you know, smoking marijuana. I just didn't care," McCarthy said. "I had no interest in being a good kid. I come from a good family, a very good family and I just wanted to waste it all away. I didn't care."

Crangle asked about McCarthy's strained relationship with his family.

"So, you don't want to bother them much?"

"I do, but I don't, you know what I mean? They have their own lives," McCarthy said. Again, the transcript redacted comments before he added, "I don't want them to see that. You know, and their kids are grown up now so it kind of drove a wedge between us. But at the same time when I look at it, they are like, 'Do you need anything?' And I say, 'No, I don't.' I don't need much."

Crangle returned to asking about prison life.
"How long have you been at Groveland for?"
"I want to say four or five months, maybe."
"Where were you before that, the last prison?"
The question, seemingly routine, prompted McCarthy to claim mistreatment by corrections officers at Cayuga Correctional Facility.
"That's in my folder.... There was some serious, serious business going on there that was not good," McCarthy said, adding that the "COs tried to set me up.... They just kept stealing my stuff. I was assaulted. They cut me."
McCarthy said he tried to report this abuse to the Office of Special Investigations, the investigative arm of DOCCS, including how officers brought copies of "A Stranger Killed Katy" into the prison.
McCarthy singled out one officer by name, although the transcript redacted it. "That book that's in your possession, he brought that into the prison system, and he gave it to guys in the dorm and let them read it."
"Is that how you found out that there was such a book?" Lee asked.
"Yes."
"Oh, I see. How many years ago was that?"
"Less than six months ago." In other words, McCarthy was claiming he didn't know a book about his murder of Katy existed until about two years after it was published.
McCarthy returned to accusations against the officers.
"And I was cut," he said. "I was assaulted. I was cut. All my property was stolen, everything. Even all my legal work was stolen."
This drew Commissioner Coppola into his first questions of the hearing.
"You said an officer brought the book into the prison?" he asked.
"Absolutely."
"And that's when you became aware of the book?"
"Absolutely," McCarthy said.
Coppola asked when McCarthy learned the book was in his file.
"When I reviewed my parole folder—don't hold me on this date," he said. "But I believe it was like three weeks ago, maybe a month ago that I reviewed my parole file, and I was aware that the book was submitted."

That would make it late May that McCarthy spotted it in his file.

"Did you read the book?" Coppola asked.

"No. It's all lies," McCarthy said.

"How do you know?" Coppola asked. "Did you read it? Wait. You just said you didn't read it."

"People have told me."

"Well, no, no, no. It's not that simple," Coppola said.

"My lawyer read the book," McCarthy said, apparently referring to Kates. "My fiancée read the book. They told me it is all a bunch of lies."

"Well, that's what they told you. You don't know that because you didn't read it," Coppola said. "When did your lawyer read it?"

"I am not sure."

"When did your fiancée read it?"

"I am not sure. She doesn't tell me everything she does."

"When was the book published? I don't even know," Coppola said.

"I have no idea," McCarthy said. "It was published by a guy who went to the same high school that I did."

"So how are you objecting to something that you don't even know about?" Coppola said.

"Because I am aware of the book."

Coppola explained that, as a parole commissioner, people often wrote things about him; he wouldn't describe their writings as lies without reading them. Coppola hadn't read "A Stranger Killed Katy," he said, but he guessed correctly it drew heavily on parole hearing transcripts.

"So, what you are saying is, if those things are in the book, it's all lies," Coppola said. "If there were, then what you are saying is the court reporters that work for us, they are lying?"

McCarthy backtracked a little. "Okay. I won't say they are all lies, but the majority of the book is based on a lie."

Coppola wasn't ready to let McCarthy off the hook.

"Okay. So, but you said you know this because your lawyer read it, and your fiancée read it, and they told you about it and if—"

McCarthy interrupted. "No. They didn't tell me about the book," he said. "Excuse me. Let me rephrase that wording. They told me that the contents of the book are built on lies."

Coppola sought clarification. "Who is 'they'?"

"My fiancée and my lawyer."

"Okay," Coppola said. "And when do you think they told you that?"

"I can't put a timeframe on that," McCarthy said.

"Come on. Six months ago, a year ago, last time you met me?" Coppola asked, referring to the April 2021 parole hearing.

"If you are going to hold me for a date—"

"No. I am not holding you," Coppola said. "Give me an approximate. I am not going to hold you to it."

"I don't know," McCarthy said. "I can't pinpoint that. I have other things that I am trying to do. That book is not one of them."

Coppola wasn't buying that McCarthy was too busy to care about the book. He noted McCarthy had spent the beginning of the hearing requesting a postponement to find a legal way to have the book removed from his file.

"That you want that (book) out of the file so that we don't review it or consider it or whatever—I get that. Don't get me wrong, I do get that," Coppola said.

"Okay."

"So, I get it like you don't want those negative things," Coppola said. "But what I am saying to you is, I am just curious. Give me a guesstimate of—you said that they read it and they told you it's all lies or fabrications or whatever you want to call it and—"

"About a year and a half ago," McCarthy said, answering the question before Coppola could ask it again.

With that, McCarthy revised his story to say he first knew about "A Stranger Killed Katy" in early 2022, a year after it was published. (Kates declined in 2025 to confirm McCarthy's claim that she said the book was "a bunch of lies," and McCarthy's fiancée did not respond to a request for an interview.)

Coppola asked again when McCarthy discovered the book in his file.

"I am not even going to put a date on it, because I don't remember," McCarthy said.

"Yeah. But we have to."

"5/17.

"5/17," Coppola repeated. "So that's a month and ten days ago. You had all that time to put in writing that you wanted a postponement to challenge this book. Why didn't you do it then?"

"Because I was in the law library trying to find out if it is challengeable."

"So, what did you find out?" Coppola asked.

"No. I can't get in the law library because the way the facility—I am not making excuses."

Coppola pointed out that McCarthy earlier had mentioned his schedule included going to the law library.

"A lot. Not every day, but a lot," McCarthy said.

"No. No. Come on. Now you just told me that it's hard to get into the law library."

"It is hard to get in."

"In the past 30 days, how many times have you been in the law library?"

"Oh, 15 maybe," McCarthy said. "Maybe 18."

Coppola wanted to know why McCarthy cared whether the book was in his file if it contained a bunch of lies.

"Because it is swaying your decision on releasing or denying my release. That's why," McCarthy said.

Coppola pressed McCarthy to explain why he didn't put in writing his request for a hearing delay in May when he learned the book was in his file.

"Because I wasn't concerned about it when I found it was in my file. When I started researching it in the law library, that's when I found out, wait a minute, there is some legislation to be concerned about here, and I can't get to the law library because of the way the rec schedule runs here."

Coppola started to say something, but McCarthy cut him off with a complaint how there was one law-library typewriter for 600 inmates, and how "they don't let you out for recreation because there's issues at this facility," and "you can only get to the law library at certain times."

Coppola reminded McCarthy he had plenty of time to put his objection to the book in writing by the deadline.

If there was anyone who knew the rules inside out, Coppola suggested, it was McCarthy. The commissioner noted that records of McCarthy's contact with prison staff show that he was extremely knowledgeable in preparing his parole file.

"So, you are—you had way more ample time within that 10-day period to ask for a postponement. You did," he said.

"Okay."

"And you never put it in the file. There's a reason that that's a strong policy. There's a reason for that. I am not expecting you to understand the reason, but I think that you know."

Before passing questioning back to Lee, Coppola pulled out a transcript from the 2019 hearing during which McCarthy said Coppola's questions made him look "at things I never looked at before." Coppola pointed out this was essentially the same thing McCarthy had just said about Lee.

"So, I mean, you have been in prison for a long, long time," Coppola said, leaving McCarthy to get the point that, by 2023, he shouldn't be relying on a parole board to make him confront reality.

McCarthy sidestepped a direct response.

"Okay. Mr. Coppola, I have been exposed to some pretty good programs, and it makes me think the way that I conclude things from the history of what I have done, the heinous crime that I committed, and I try to look at in it a sense that it is logical. Yes, it was a bad crime. Am I trying to be honest? Absolutely."

McCarthy sensed Coppola was beginning to interrupt.

"Let me finish now," McCarthy pleaded.

"I didn't say anything," Coppola said.

"You started to. Did you not?"

"No. I am breathing."

"All right. Don't breathe. Don't breathe," McCarthy said.

Coppola remained silent.

"So," McCarthy said, "the things that I am looking at I am trying to answer in a logical way after remembering what happened.... You are asking me questions that are making me think: Are these the things that I really want to say, or are these the things that I really want to just blurt out because I am not trying to hide anything? I am trying to be as truthful as I can."

McCarthy seemed to be suggesting that he provided answers without fully thinking because he didn't want to be seen as evasive.

After encouraging McCarthy to just tell the truth, Coppola returned to the events of August 29, 1986, and McCarthy's claim that Katy spit at him because he couldn't perform sexually.

"How did you know at that point she was saying that you couldn't perform? What was exactly happening? I don't mean to be disgusting, but I need to ask," Coppola said.

"Physically I couldn't perform," McCarthy answered.

"You attempted to penetrate her, and you are saying you couldn't do it?"

"No. I didn't say that."

"So, what are you saying you couldn't perform? At what point does she know that you can't perform? I don't get it," Coppola said.

McCarthy said he wasn't "excited."

"How did she know? You weren't naked. How did she know?"

"It's not too hard to tell."

"I will let it be very clear. How did she know that you couldn't perform?"

"Because I didn't have the physical ability to perform."

No matter how many ways Coppola phrased the question, McCarthy wasn't giving any kind of explicit answer.

"Okay," Coppola said. "You told Commissioner Lee that she [Katy] was not naked, that she was maybe in the process of taking off her clothes."

"Right."

"Well, you couldn't perform. She was taking off her clothes, you didn't start to have sex. Why should she be taking off her clothes?"

"She was trying to entice me. She was trying to get me excited so that we could have sex," McCarthy said.

"So, she was the aggressor here?"

"No."

"You killed her, but she was the aggressor?" Coppola asked.

"No. It was mutual."

Coppola said it almost sounded to him like McCarthy was claiming Katy was forcing herself on him.

"No. It was mutual because we both agreed upon to have sex, but when I couldn't perform, that's when she got disgusted."

"Yes, but wait," Coppola said. "You said she got disgusted, she spit at you, whatever, but you are saying that she tried to continue to entice you?"

"Right," McCarthy said.

"If she already knew you couldn't, at what point did she end up spitting at you?"

"Well, I don't know if she really realized it wasn't going to happen," McCarthy said, "but sometimes you just keep trying and trying, and I was like, 'I can't perform, I can't do anything. I am not physically capable of having intercourse.' I don't know if it was because I was too drunk or what it was. I don't know."

McCarthy indicated he pleaded guilty to attempted rape not because he sexually assaulted Katy but because she died, and he needed "to redeem any quality that I have left from being scum."

If that admission of guilt is "the attribute that everybody looks at, if that's the way that things are held against me, I don't know what else to say," he said.

"Okay."

McCarthy once again blurted out, "There's no DNA. Show me. So, there's no intercourse," as if that was proof he was telling the truth.

Finally, Coppola had enough. The commissioner stated that a reasonable person could conclude McCarthy was lying about having a prior relationship with Katy and about her agreeing to have sex with him outside the arena.

"I know…that you object to anybody with the belief that you're exaggerating your relationship with her," Coppola told McCarthy. "Well, guess what? It's a 'reasonable probability.' That is what they call it: a reasonable probability that maybe you are not telling the truth when it comes to this consensual agreement."

Coppola noted that there was no corroborating evidence to back up McCarthy's claims that Katy agreed to have sex.

"There's no record other than you and her, what you say now. And as I told you before, she is not here to defend herself that there was no consensual agreement to have sex," the commissioner said. "Well, guess what? If nobody knows, it is reasonable to think that maybe somebody else is exaggerating the facts. That's reasonable."

"If that's what you think, Mr. Coppola," McCarthy said.

"No, it's not what I think," Coppola said, emphasizing that it's just a reasonable opinion not to believe McCarthy had a relationship with Katy.

"I don't see where the word relationship keeps coming up," McCarthy said, apparently forgetting that he stated at the 2011 hearing that he and Katy had "an intimate relationship" prior to the night he attacked her.

McCarthy insisted that he had no motive to lie.

Coppola argued that indeed he did.

"The motive is to make it sound like...(you) didn't try to rape her and kill her. That's the motive. To make it not sound like this was a random act of violence. Not that it escalated to the violence, but it was a random act, that maybe you did see her from a distance, and you liked her."

Coppola said, though, he wasn't claiming McCarthy was lying.

"I wasn't there," he said.

McCarthy once again claimed, rather than being a liar, he suffered a faulty memory and an inability to always express himself clearly.

"Sometimes it's a little hard for me to remember some of the things that I have done," McCarthy said. "Some of the things are even more difficult to try to express it. I don't have the opportunity in here. I don't speak to many people in here at all. I kind of stay to myself. I have a lot of self-reflection because I know I did some serious hurt to a lot of people. Not just [redacted], but I did a lot of hurt to a lot of people in the community, especially my family and her family.

"I try to look at it in the sense that I am trying to recover or repair the damage that I caused. And some of the questions that you asked me, some of them really have a lot of hurt that cause other people harm, not just me. So, I try to be truthful, but I am trying to be as soft as I can."

And then, before Coppola or any other commissioner could ask what being "soft" meant, McCarthy returned to his complaint about "A Stranger Killed Katy" while denying he was doing so.

"Not to get off on (the) topic, I am not talking about the book again. This guy went to the same school that I did, [redacted]," he said.

"I don't know. Who is [redacted]?" Coppola asked.

"The guy that wrote that book, [redacted]," McCarthy said. "He wrote to me, and he tried to get personal with me. He tried to trick me because he wanted to befriend me and come and visit me, and I wrote a letter to him. I don't know if it's in the book or not, but I wrote a letter to him and said, no, thank you, [redacted]. I prefer not to because I think it is going to cause the family more harm than it will do anything else.

"And I understand that he wrote the book trying to slam me. He wrote the book to try to make my crime look worse than it really is," McCarthy said.

Quickly, he backtracked: "I don't think you can. It was the most heinous crime in my opinion. I wasn't raised that, nor would I think that way."

But the damage was already done. The commissioners said nothing about McCarthy's revealing slip of the tongue in which he claimed that the book exaggerated his murder of Katy. One obvious conclusion was that, deep down, McCarthy didn't believe his crime was as bad as what he pleaded guilty to committing—and, in his mind, he was the real victim here.

McCarthy continued by addressing Coppola directly.

"Some of the questions you've asked me were pretty tough," McCarthy said. "So, you have given me an opportunity to think about it. Granted, you are probably going to hit me for two years, and I will see you in two years."

Coppola replied, "We haven't discussed it, and remember, Commissioner Crangle—"

"That's the same thing you said last time," McCarthy said of Coppola previously stating the board didn't make up its mind before deliberating.

"Well, no. But that's the truth," Coppola said. "We are bound by law. We never talk about what we want to do or how we feel about something until it's all over with. And that would be illegal, and I for one would never do that."

Coppola pointed out that the commissioners don't always agree on whether to grant parole.

"We disagreed a couple times today already," he said, apparently referring to other hearings on the agenda.

McCarthy responded with a resigned, "That's all right."

By this point, the proceedings had stretched to more than four times the 15-minute average duration of a New York parole hearing. Yet, there was no sign that the commissioners were running out of questions.

Commissioner Lee shifted the discussion to the day in St. Lawrence County Court in 1987 when the judge sent McCarthy off to prison.

"Mr. McCarthy, what do you remember about your sentencing date? What stands out in your mind?"

"Say that one more time for me, Commissioner Lee."

"What stands out most about your sentencing date on September 11th, 1987? I mean—"

McCarthy stopped her midsentence.

"The amount of people that were standing behind me that I hurt," he said.

"And who would that be?"

"Pretty much the entire college and community campus."

"Okay," she said. "Because I think this was a—like the crime of the century in this little college town."

"It was. It was very bad."

Lee then read aloud Judge Nicandri's statement at sentencing, which detailed how McCarthy had pleaded guilty to second-degree murder committed while "attempting to engage in sexual intercourse with [redacted] who was at the time incapable of consenting to an act of intercourse by reason of her being physically helpless." She also quoted the judge as stating McCarthy admitted that he caused Katy's death by strangling her.

"Do you remember that?" Lee asked.

"No, I don't," McCarthy said.

"That's a big difference than what you said about (the crime) during this interview to me," Lee stated.

McCarthy offered no response, and Lee continued.

She noted that, at sentencing, the judge entered into the record a letter from McCarthy to the probation department. Lee expressed curiosity about what McCarthy meant in his letter when he stated that his constitutional rights were being violated.

"I don't remember," McCarthy said.

"You don't remember?"

"I do not."

"Okay," Lee said. "Do you remember saying that your 'constitutional rights have been violated with lies in the newspapers headlines, perjury from the chief of police officials for personal benefits in the areas of justification.' What was that all about?"

"They said that I had some DWIs on my record," McCarthy said.

"I am sorry. What?"

McCarthy claimed that deputies who transported him from the county jail to the courthouse taunted him, saying they could insert false information into his record. However, he offered no explanation for why this allegation wasn't stated in his letter, which implied there was perjurious testimony against him.

"So, what's that have to do with this case?" Lee said of the letter. "Do you think you were unlawfully arrested on this case?"

"No. Absolutely not."

Lee then turned to McCarthy's presentencing report, which the parole board knew he had seen since he went to court in 2009 to obtain a copy.

"Now, when you got arrested," Lee began, "you did not initially confess that you killed her, right? You tried to lay the blame on some third person, right? Is that true?"

"Well, when I was hit in the back of the head—I was trying to explain that I was there with a third person, yes," McCarthy said.

"Okay," Lee said. "So, you portrayed yourself as a victim, and then this unidentified third person was the one who did all of this to you and the victim?"

"That's your words," McCarthy said, adding that he wasn't sure what he said because "whatever documents were submitted to you, I haven't seen them all because I am not privy to all that information."

The presentencing report also quoted McCarthy as saying he "discovered the girl in a semiconscious state."

"Do you remember saying that?" Lee asked.

"No, I do not," McCarthy said.

"And when they asked you about the letter that you wrote, right?" Lee said, referring to the statement the judge read aloud at sentencing. "It says something like, you did what you had to do to survive. What was that all about?"

"Something to survive?"

Lee dug out a copy.

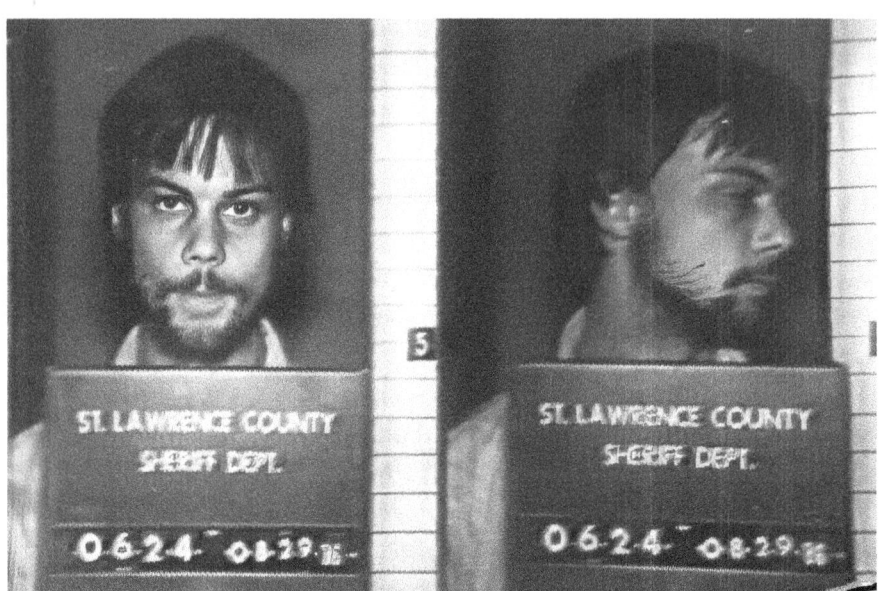

Brian McCarthy appears in mug shots taken on August 29, 1986, at the St. Lawrence County Jail, shortly after his arraignment for the assault on Katy Hawelka. (St. Lawrence County Sheriff's Department photo.)

"Oh, here," she said. "When you were questioned by the investigator on the accuracy of your statement to the court, a handwritten letter by you, you acknowledged, 'Everyone has their own beliefs.'"

The investigator also wrote that, when McCarthy was asked about his statement, he claimed he "is trying to survive."

Lee asked what McCarthy meant about "trying to survive."

"That's a really strange response when you were asked about the accuracy of your statement. Do you have a copy of that letter?"

"I do not."

"Okay."

"Ma'am," McCarthy said, "all my property, all my legal material, everything that I had was stolen from me after I was transferred and assaulted, and I don't have any reference to any documents. So, I had to try to get documents. I have been trying—"

McCarthy paused, sensing Lee was ready to interrupt.

"Let me finish, please, Ms. Lee," he said. "I have tried to acquire the documents that I had before. Some has taken me years to get, and it was taken from me. So, I don't have reference to the stuff that you are talking about."

"Okay. I see."

"All right."

The transcript redactions that followed left it unclear whether McCarthy explained who had allegedly taken his documents, or why their absence prevented him from remembering contents of those he had decades to read over and over.

Lee invited McCarthy to talk about some of the goals listed in his case plan.

"You said you wanted to develop better coping skills—tasks to learn to avoid situations before it gets out of hand," she said. "What do you mean by that?"

"Everyday life," McCarthy answered. "Everybody has anger. How do you deal with it? Instead of just acting on it, I want to be able to deal with it and walk away or not act on it at all. I want to be able to compensate for whatever I've learned and use those tools in such an environment as this."

McCarthy said he made a point in prison to learn coping and other skills, even teaching himself sign language.

As McCarthy spoke about prison life, Crangle was still intrigued by what McCarthy had said earlier in the hearing about being under the influence on the morning Katy was killed.

After Lee turned over the questioning to Crangle, he asked: "You admitted that it was alcohol and possibly even some marijuana, right?"

"Yeah. I think there were other drugs, too. I don't remember," McCarthy said.

Crangle asked if it was possible McCarthy was so drunk "that you don't remember everything, and the fact that you initiated to try to rape her and she didn't want to, and that's why you punched her?"

"No. I don't think that's—I am telling you, I didn't punch anybody. It was a knee-jerk reaction."

"Okay. Well, the knee-jerk reaction was a hit."

"Right."

Crangle then suggested that maybe McCarthy's inability to perform sexually was due to Katy not wanting sex, and then "you got mad and that's what you did."

"Maybe you couldn't perform because she was unwilling to perform?" the commissioner asked.

"That is a possibility, yes," McCarthy said.

Without commenting on Crangle's theories, Commissioner Coppola spoke up, making it clear he wasn't buying McCarthy's claim that all he did was strike Katy once as a knee-jerk reaction. Coppola noted the autopsy report stated "the actual cause of death was strangulation" after she was beaten unconscious.

"Okay," McCarthy said. "I will go with that. Whatever you say. Whatever you say, Mr. Coppola."

"No. So you—"

McCarthy interrupted. "I tried to express to you that I don't have those documents anymore. I can't refer to those documents."

"Listen, I am not lying to you," Coppola said of the autopsy report. "We can read it to you. We have it."

"You are asking me a question," McCarthy said, "and you want an answer and the answer is 'yes.'"

At that point, Coppola made it clear he had enough of McCarthy's claims that he had memory loss, or that someone stole his documents, or that he didn't know what was in his file, or that he didn't have time to prepare.

"Let me give you some advice in your learning every day," Coppola said. "You are not coping very well because—"

"No," McCarthy said. "Because I am a little frustrated because you are asking me questions that I can't possibly answer because I don't have the documents in front of me."

Coppola said that excuse didn't make sense.

"Okay. But I am telling you that we can refer" to the documents, Coppola said before returning to his advice. "See, here's where you are not coping well."

McCarthy started to interrupt again, but this time Coppola cut him off.

"You are not letting me finish," the commissioner said. "You don't even know where I am going with this."

"Okay," McCarthy said.

"You are automatically jumping in (saying), 'I don't know. I don't see the records. I don't have this.' But let me tell you something," Coppola said. "I believe you know a lot more than what's in your file than you are letting us believe, because you know this file backwards and forwards. Everything that you are allowed by law to see, you have seen. Trust me, I know that."

Coppola had seen in McCarthy's file multiple memos from prison staff making it clear McCarthy had rigorously studied its contents.

"So, I don't want to get into that game of: 'I don't know what you are looking at'," Coppola said.

As he was speaking, Lee pulled up McCarthy's presentencing report.

"Manual strangulation. That's what it says in the PSI, okay?" Lee said, holding up her hands to demonstrate a choking grasp. "You keep referring to this knee-jerk reaction, and I get it." However, she said, the autopsy report showed "her [Katy] being beaten unconscious and then strangled. That is not a knee-jerk reaction."

McCarthy insisted he had no memory of strangling Katy.

"I don't remember if I did," he said. "If I did, I did. If that shows—if the physical evidence shows, the medical examination shows—then I did."

Lee thanked him for that concession.

"I am not denying that. I am saying there are things that I don't remember," McCarthy said.

The transcript redacted the next few comments, although it appeared McCarthy returned to blaming the murder of Katy on his anger over being sexually molested as a child.

"Being that I took that out on that poor girl, shame on me," he said.

Despite McCarthy's seven parole denials since 2009, Lee made it clear the door wasn't permanently closed.

"So, Mr. McCarthy, what challenges do you think you will face if and when you are released back to the community?" she asked. "Have you ever thought about that?"

"Yes, I have. Every day I think about that."

She asked him to list those challenges.

"If society will ever accept me. If I am ever going to be able to walk down the street without getting killed," McCarthy said. "If I am going to have an issue with being able to be employed. If I am going to be able to interact with people. If I am going to be able to have an opportunity to actually do something for the rest of my life other than be in prison."

"What else?"

"If I am able to repay, if I am able to recover and redeem myself in society's eyes so that I can do something good. I want to try to make things right."

Lee wanted to know if McCarthy thought his incarceration for nearly 37 years was sufficient punishment.

"No."

"Why not?"

"Pretty obvious answer."

"I don't know. I want to hear your side of the story, why you think that's the case," Lee said.

"I created a pretty bad scene. I created a lot of disturbance in a lot of people's lives."

Lee asked if he thought justice was served for himself or Katy's family.

"No, I do not," he said.

Asked to explain, McCarthy replied, "Because I don't think the family was given justice because they lost their daughter."

"What kind of impact do you think it will have on the victim's family if you are released back to the community?" Lee asked. "Have you ever thought about that?"

"They will be outraged. I have thought about it."

"Why do you think that's the case?" Lee asked.

"Because it was such a bad crime," McCarthy said.

After another heavily redacted exchange, McCarthy insisted that he had never intentionally lied to the parole board.

"I tried to give you the best answers that I can, Ms. Lee, and I try to be as truthful as I can. Sometimes my memory fails me. Did I commit a bad crime? Absolutely. I would be a fool to think that I didn't."

And he made sure to emphasize that he stayed informed, even tracking the number of people who signed the family's petition opposing his parole.

"56,000 signatures against my release is quite a big—quite a few signatures on the petition, however the petition is written," McCarthy said. "Like Mr. Coppola said, I do my research, and I try to be up to date on what's going on, and I am trying to be as truthful to you as I possibly can. Whether I am a little bit cloudy on some of the stuff, yes. I am trying."

"Do you think that your memory improves as time passes on?" Lee asked.

"No, I don't," he said. "I think my memory is fading as I get older.…I am in pretty good shape, but my mind, because I don't have the stimulation in here, I don't have the stimulus mind. In here you have a bunch of addicts and dope fiends, and I don't like interacting with them."

Perhaps concerned the commissioners might think he was saying he was better than his fellow inmates, McCarthy was quick to add, "Show me someone else that has a more heinous crime."

Lee indicated she was wrapping up the hearing, but she first wanted to ask about McCarthy's suggestion that he kept files on commissioners Crangle and Coppola.

"What do you mean by files? What files are you talking about?"

McCarthy said he had been referring to the commissioners' official bios posted by DOCCS online.

"Okay. Gotcha," she said.

"You, too, Commissioner Lee. They put these on the NYS website," he said. "Well, it is just a bio of your history, your education, the people that you interact with. But just like you know me, I want to try to get to understand who you are, too, so I can try to communicate with you."

"All right. Sir, anything else?" Lee asked.

"I want to appreciate the great consideration for the time that you have given me," he answered. "I know that you have little to no belief in what I am trying to tell you based on what the records are, and you are probably not going to release me based on such a heinous crime, but I appreciate you giving me the opportunity."

Lee pointed out that Commissioner Coppola had already told him that he was wrong to imply the commissioners already had their minds made up before they completed the interview.

"You are kind of alluding that, you know, this is like—you know, I am a little offended by your statement," she said.

"I am sorry."

That reminded Lee that McCarthy had also made an accusation implying misconduct by G. Kevin Ludlow, who as a commissioner had met with Katy's brother, Joe, for an impact statement.

"Oh, yeah," McCarthy said. "That's right. I forgot about that. He got a statement from the brother. He's the lead opposition to my release, and I don't blame him a bit, but at the same time Officer Ludlow interviewed him and got a statement from him. I forgot all about that. You have a pretty good memory."

With that, Coppola spoke up again.

"So, because you are so thorough, and you do your homework about us —"

"Oh, here we go. Here we go," McCarthy said.

"I know that you know the section of the law that we work under."

"259-i," McCarthy stated.

"Backwards and forwards. You probably know it better than us, backwards and forwards," Coppola said. "You put in an appeal on every case. I know that you know it. I know your attorney knows it. So, I know that you know that part of our job, we get paid to do this, right? That means we must do certain things. Part of our job requires us when scheduled to meet with victims or their representative when the victim is unable."

"I know," McCarthy said.

Coppola was just getting started. He wanted McCarthy to know how wrong it was to imply there was a conflict of interest for Ludlow or any other commissioner to meet with Katy's family members.

"We meet thousands of victims. We are required to do that. That's part of our job. We have to, even if we didn't want to," Coppola said.

While Coppola didn't believe he had taken an impact statement from Katy's family, he said, having done so wouldn't disqualify him from sitting on one of McCarthy's parole hearings or joining in the decision.

As for McCarthy implying the board already made up its mind about him, Coppola said, "you jump to a lot of conclusions."

The commissioner pointed out that the board in the past has granted parole to numerous inmates convicted of murder.

"And you have seen some of those people go home, right?" Coppola asked.

"I have. One of them just recently," McCarthy said.

"And guess what? I can guarantee that I was one of the votes that might have sent some of those people home. So, to jump to the conclusion that Commissioner Crangle, myself, or Commissioner Lee have a foregone conclusion on your case before we have even had a chance to discuss it—"

"No. You are right," McCarthy said. "It is wrong of me to assume that."

With that, Lee thanked McCarthy for attending the hearing, and for sitting through a "very lengthy interview." It lasted so long, she said, because "we had a lot to cover (and) because, like I said, I spent hours and hours on your file."

"Thank you," McCarthy said. "I am sorry you had to go through that and relive that horrific crime that I committed. I appreciate your time, and I hope that there are things that I can have in the future that will give me some kind of comfort, as well as the family comfort."

Lee said he could expect to receive a decision in a few days.

"Best of luck to you, sir," she said.

"Thank you," McCarthy said. "Thank you. Thank you. Thank you."

With that, the hearing was over. The transcript didn't include its exact duration. But based on its 120 pages, the hearing lasted well over an hour, possibly even two, easily the longest one for McCarthy. By comparison, his past hearing transcripts ran 23 pages in 2009, 11 in 2011, 13 in 2013, 15 in 2015, 19 in 2017, 64 in 2019, and 43 in 2021.

On July 12, 2023, Katy's family posted the parole board's decision on their Facebook page:

> PAROLE DENIED. We are thrilled that Justice will continue for our sweet, beloved Katy....The sentence was 23 years to life and that is exactly the time this convicted murderer should serve - LIFE in prison."

The commissioners' vote to deny parole was 3-0. In its partially redacted decision, the board told McCarthy he had taken positive steps by completing mandatory prison programs, working as a porter, and keeping a clean disciplinary record since his last hearing in 2021.

On the other hand, the commissioners found McCarthy tried to "minimize" his crime by claiming he hit Katy just once while attempting to engage in consensual sex, a version that conflicted with the record. They added:

> The instant offense is a continuation and escalation of your unlawful behavior. The panel was particularly disturbed by your willingness to commit this horrific crime while you were under probation....
>
> Furthermore, you stated you had remorse but your actions were extremely violent, egregious and heinous demonstrating your poor judgment. You took the life of [redacted] a college student who did not have an opportunity to finish college and fulfill her dreams and goals in her life because you killed her....
>
> After consideration of all factors, to grant your discretionary release at this time would so deprecate the serious nature of your crime as to undermine respect for the law and would so trivialize a loss of life. Parole is denied.

The commissioners set McCarthy's next parole eligibility date in 2025 when he would be 62.

The DOCCS website listing decisions in parole appeals, as of mid-February 2025, showed no record of McCarthy filing one in 2023.

McCarthy would spend several more months at Groveland before the corrections department transferred him downstate to Otisville Correctional Facility. There he would remain incarcerated at the time this book was published, shortly before his ninth parole hearing in April 2025.

Chapter 8

'It's Never Going to End for Us'

In the fall of 2023, Terry Taber sat on her sofa, hands clenched in her lap, sharing her Syracuse living room with a TV news crew. Terry was always happy to talk about her beloved Katy, even if these interviews came at a price. They meant bringing up the man who not only killed Terry's second-oldest daughter but had spent the past 14 years attempting to rewrite the narrative of how it happened.

On Terry's right sat Katy's siblings: Joe Jr. and Carey; on the left, Betsy. On the coffee table nearby lay a spread of photos—Katy as a little girl, Katy in her prom dress, Katy at her Henninger High School graduation. In many, her big 1980s hair was perfectly teased, and her radiant smile reflected the happiness and optimism of a young woman looking forward to a bright future.

A camera from WNYT-TV (Channel 13) from Albany zoomed in on Betsy's hand cradling a gold-colored Pulsar watch, its band broken. It was the watch Katy wore the morning Brian McCarthy beat, kicked and strangled her. For Betsy, the band had come to symbolize so many broken dreams. It also was a tangible reminder of why she and her family continued to make impact statements.

"You may have someone who's admitted guilt in our case, and, you know, is committed to an institution," Betsy told Channel 13 reporter Stella Porter. "But then, you know, it never ends. It's never going to end for us."

Terry and Katy's siblings had placed themselves in this kind of media spotlight on and off since 2009 in hopes the appearances stirred support for their petition opposing McCarthy's parole.

Katy Hawelka's family is interviewed for a two-part news report that aired in November 2023 on Albany's WNYT-TV (Channel 13). From left, Joe Hawelka Jr., Carey Patton, Terry Taber, and Betsy McInerney. (WNYT-TV photo.)

Recently, Porter pointed out, the family also advocated for Lorraine's Law, the proposed state legislation aimed at increasing the time between parole hearings for some inmates convicted of murder. The legislation was intended to give victims' families a greater opportunity to rebuild their lives without the constant disruption and trauma of a hearing every 24 months.

Referring to the months before a hearing, Carey said, "In December, we get through the holidays, and it's like, all right, starting in January, we have to start thinking about this again."

Joe Hawelka Jr. was just 17 years old in 1987 when McCarthy was sent to prison for Katy's murder. Back then, it was hard for Katy's brother to grasp that one day her killer would be eligible for parole.

"Twenty-three years felt like forever," Joe said of his teenage perspective. "At that age, it seemed like a lifetime."

But it wasn't. McCarthy was 46 years old in 2009 when he became eligible for parole, with a chance to grow old outside of prison. To Katy's family, it seemed so cruelly unfair—and dangerous. They feared that, if released, he would hurt someone else the same way he hurt Katy.

So they pored over the unsettling and anger-inducing transcripts from each one of McCarthy's parole hearings. They set up a Facebook page asking strangers to sign the family's petition opposing his parole. They met with a commissioner every two years to discuss Katy and to draw attention to the lies and inconsistencies they spotted in McCarthy's previous parole testimony.

Giving an impact statement always was traumatic, Terry said, as it sent her mind back to August 29, 1986, when a telephone call from the Potsdam police chief sent her and Katy's father rushing to their daughter's side at a Watertown hospital, where the teenager died September 1 without regaining consciousness.

Each impact statement, Terry told Channel 13, "brings everything back to the day that it happened and getting that call at 5 in the morning and rushing up to…(the hospital) and finding my daughter, (and discovering) that her father didn't recognize her (because) she had been beaten so badly."

With each new parole hearing, it was like that horrible day "starts all over again," Terry said.

At the same time, Carey said, she was convinced that McCarthy hardly gave Katy a second thought until the commissioners started asking him questions.

"After his first parole hearing, we got a copy of the transcript. He didn't know my sister's name. He'd been in prison, and didn't even know who he murdered," Carey said.

In the television interview, the way Carey's voice broke slightly when talking about Katy revealed as much about their bond as the words.

"She was one of my best friends in high school," Carey said. "And she was the peacemaker. Growing up, you know, four kids in the house and we would be fighting, and she would always be the one to be like, 'Let's get along. Let's.' So, she was very special."

On August 28, 1986, Katy packed up the family car and pointed it north to Potsdam, with Terry and Carey along for the ride. Katy was ready to take on her sophomore year, hit the books hard, and make her mark there.

"Very studious, serious about her studies, was looking forward to Clarkson University," Betsy said.

:RT HARDY   KATHERINE M. HAWELKA   LEE ROGER HEN|
             "Katy"   "Glow"

Katy Hawelka in the 1985 yearbook for Henninger High School in Syracuse, New York.

Hours later, security guards would find Katy unconscious near a Clarkson pathway, beaten and strangled by a stranger who had no legitimate reason to be on campus. While her family still grappled with their loss decades later, McCarthy spent his time coming up with strategies to get out of prison.

"So how in the world could he be eligible for parole?" Betsy asked. "And why do we have to go through this every 24 months?"

The Channel 13 interview aired in November 2023 as part of a two-day report on Lorraine's Law, with Katy's family speaking up for those who saw it as a common-sense solution.

"I don't understand why the legislature in Albany keeps fighting it," Terry said.

The best explanation was that advocates for prisoner rights and parole reform had lobbied hard against Lorraine's Law. They argued it would be unfair to inmates who have shown they changed while in prison.

At present, even a two-year gap between parole hearings can seem excruciatingly long for an inmate waiting for another chance, activist Gordon Davis told Channel 13. A convicted murderer who was granted parole in 2020, Davis now worked in Albany with at-risk youths.

Lorraine's Law, he said, would set back recent efforts to make sure the parole board didn't look solely at the horrific nature of the crime.

"We have lawyers, we have doctors, we have psychiatrists on the parole board now. So, it's like, we're going to look at the whole picture," Davis said. "But now y'all say y'all want to redo all this again and make it a harder chance for a person to go before the parole board?"

The way Betsy saw it, though, those seeking to liberalize the parole system want people to believe that every inmate can be rehabilitated, that everyone behind bars should eventually be freed.

"Now there's a lot of conversation about reform," she told Channel 13. "Brian McCarthy has never been reformed."

Melanie Trimble stood at an Albany rally in early December 2024, carrying a sign reading, "Free Our Elderly." Nearby, a protester sported a black sweatshirt with the words "Release Aging People in Prison."

Trimble, regional director for the New York Civil Liberties Union in the Capital Region, was among those calling for the New York State Legislature to pass the "Elder Parole" bill, which would grant a parole board interview to incarcerated individuals age 55 and older who have served at least 15 years. She also endorsed the "Fair and Timely Parole" bill, which would require the parole board to release eligible individuals unless their case record shows a "current and unreasonable risk" that they would violate the law if released.

"If we pass these two measures, they at least have the chance to come in and tell their stories. To show how they have been rehabilitated, to show how they are going to help the communities they are returning to," she told Albany's *Spectrum News 1* local cable news channel.

There is a good chance both bills will pass in 2025, a spokesperson for Release Aging People in Prison told New York City public-radio website *Gothamist*. Other advocates happily noted 2025 wasn't an election year, meaning politicians were more likely to support controversial parole legislation. (An aide to Governor Kathy Hochul promised only that she would review the legislation if passed by the Senate and Assembly.)

As he was nearly 63 years old, McCarthy, at least demographically, represented the type of older inmate whom parole-justice advocates wanted to help free—although, if any had singled him out for support, there was no mention of it in the public portions of hearing transcripts.

Most of that support has come from McCarthy's attorney and his fiancée, both from Upstate New York, and from a counselor priest in New Jersey.

It was mid-December 2024, and the Reverend Maximilian Buonocore found himself with ample downtime for a chat. The 67-year-old priest rested in a New Jersey hospital following October quadruple bypass surgery. A call to him at Newark Abbey was forwarded to his cellphone, which he answered with a brisk, "Father Max."

Buonocore spoke fondly of McCarthy, saying he first met him through the fiancée more than a decade ago. The priest explained that she "got to know him [McCarthy] through prison ministry that she was doing up in Ogdensburg, and got interested in his case. And then so she introduced me to him."

Even before his ordination in 2017, the priest provided counseling using his birth name, Peter P. Buonocore, under the supervision of Gerard A. Figurelli, a licensed psychologist based in Bayonne, New Jersey. Figurelli, who has provided expert testimony in court cases and conducted evaluations of inmates, has guided Buonocore's work with McCarthy. Buonocore also has a master's degree in counseling psychology from Seton Hall University. He obtained his New Jersey license for marriage and family therapy in 2012 because the state didn't want him to continue doing professional counseling without one, he said.

Buonocore acknowledged not having much experience counseling prisoners, especially ones serving time for murder. But he said he relied on guidance of Figurelli to ensure McCarthy's psychological risk evaluations were valid.

Buonocore still believed in 2024 that McCarthy was no danger to the public. The priest stuck to that conclusion even after researching McCarthy's criminal past, including reading "A Stranger Killed Katy," which

Buonocore praised for being "well-researched and well-written." He expressed happiness at being interviewed for "The Long Shadow of Katy's Killer," saying it would benefit from views of "others such as myself who have gotten to know Brian from a more interior perspective."

As far as Buonocore could tell, McCarthy has been truthful to him about his past, even revealing how he suffered sexual abuse as a teen.

"It was amazing how, you know, he achieves, was able to achieve resolution," Buonocore said.

In 2022, McCarthy arranged for Buonocore to have a Mass said in Katy's memory, which the priest viewed as a genuine expression of remorse.

At the same time, the priest said, he found himself deeply sympathetic to the grief of Katy's family and understood why they opposed McCarthy's parole.

"When I read up, I said, 'Oh, my goodness, it was horrible,' but I still felt like I wanted to work with him, and I got to know him. I guess my religious side would help me not to be repulsed, to be able to have the compassion, even though he did such a horrendous thing," Buonocore said.

He met with McCarthy several times in person, and they continued to communicate over the telephone and through email. Once he recovered from surgery, Buonocore said, it would be easier to visit McCarthy now that he was an inmate in Otisville, about 90 miles north of Newark.

Buonocore expected to continue saying Masses on his own for Katy and her family, "especially the living ones."

In late August 2024, Terry Taber stared at seven sheets of paper, folded in half and resting on a small table in her living room. The state Office of Victim Assistance had sent the pages in July after she requested all of the messages McCarthy had written to the family through the state's Apology Letter Bank.

After reading them, Terry found McCarthy's words so disturbing that she hesitated to make them available for inclusion in this book. Joe Jr. refused to even look at them, she said, while Carey suggested they be kept private, rather than allowing his lies to possibly fool others.

Ultimately, Terry decided to share the letters, believing that since McCarthy's first parole hearing in 2009, no one had done more harm to his chances of release than his own words.

"Honestly," she said of McCarthy's letters, "I think he's burying himself."

The Apology Letter Bank allows inmates to express remorse for their crimes without violating rules prohibiting direct contact with victims or their families. According to a prison directive, the letters are meant for inmates to show accountability for their crimes, to express genuine remorse, and to acknowledge the pain caused to victims and their families.

"An apology letter should not offer excuses, nor blame the victim or circumstances, such as an addiction to drugs or the age of the incarcerated individual," the directive states.

McCarthy sent his first letter to the apology bank in November 2015, but Terry didn't know it existed until two years later after he brought it up at a parole hearing. His note stated in part:

> What I want you to know is that I take full responsibility for causing the death of Kathryn (sic) and I am so very, very sorry. I am ashamed of my selfish, reckless actions caused so much pain and sorrow to you and to so many other people. …
>
> During my incarceration, I have taken several programs that led me to face my childhood demons that caused me to turn to drugs and act out my frustrations, pain and shamefulness of being sexually abused as a child. This is not an excuse for what I did, nor is this confession to you a plea for forgiveness. It is always wrong to take the life of another. I was wrong to destroy Kathryn's (sic) and your family.

To Katy's family, McCarthy's letter felt less like an apology and more like an attempt to make excuses, despite the directive's explicit prohibition of such justifications. Terry tossed the letter into a drawer and didn't read it again until it was included in "A Stranger Killed Katy."

McCarthy's next submission came on May 28, 2021, shortly after his seventh parole denial and four months after the publication of the book.

Along with his typed apology, he included a two-page "personal statement from Brian McCarthy," which he had submitted to the parole board. In it, McCarthy said he decided to "write out my true feelings about my crime" because, at past parole hearings, "often when I answer, my answers are being misconstrued." The statement also complained about the unfairness of the parole hearings:

I have tried to explain things and offer clarification on issues in the record that are misunderstood. Whenever I try to do this, it is felt that I did not show remorse or insight into my behavior. I was trying to explain certain things which have been taken out of context in the past. I have experienced having some of the same Commissioners for consecutive boards.

The statement repeated his claim that he and Katy knew each other before the murder. McCarthy implied it was Katy's fault that he told the police he didn't know her. He wrote:

One of the things I am referring to is the question of whether I knew Katy Hawelka, personally. When I was arrested and taken to the hospital, I was shown an id and I told the officers I did not know the person who was in the id. The id I was shown, was not Katy Hawelka's id. It was learned later, she had someone else's id, that she used to drink in the bar, she was at prior to the crime. She was not 21. This issue haunts me because I was only trying to explain what really happened. Throughout the years, people insist that Katy was a stranger to me. I tried to explain that I knew her in passing.

McCarthy's statement never explained why he withheld the ID story from the parole board until 2021, or why at his 1987 sentencing he conceded he didn't know Katy prior to the fatal attack.

Mostly, McCarthy's personal statement focused less on details about killing Katy, and more on how he was trying to live with himself:

I hated myself for so long. It took years to begin to understand how this could happen. I renewed my relationship with God and sought out counseling from various religious officials. I've also had mass said in her honor many times. I had to work on forgiving myself and finding a way to go on. This was not an easy task. It took a lot of soul searching to understand what happened to me.

McCarthy wrote that he had worked in prison to overcome the "demons of my youth" and to remain drug-free while finding coping mechanisms to control his anger. He concluded by expressing remorse for the pain caused others, as well as regret that the parole commissioners hadn't fully understood what he had tried to get across in the past:

> I cannot change what happened so many years ago. I wish that I could but that is not possible. My words are genuine, and I truly do feel remorse for everything that has happened as a result of my crime.
>
> Please consider my statement in addition to the hearing as I feel that due to the high pressure I feel when I appear before the board that my true feelings are not being adequately conveyed.

McCarthy's accompanying letter to the apology bank brought up his past substance abuse, claimed he had worked hard to be a better person, and insisted the family was wrong that he hadn't shown remorse. He wrote:

> I am writing this letter to express to you my extreme remorse and sorrow for the pain I caused by taking your family member from you because of my actions. I do not expect you to forgive me, but it is my hope that by receiving this letter it could bring you some peace. It is not my intention to cause further grief.
>
> Despite what you may believe, I do have remorse for my actions. I sought out counseling through clergy members and attended various rehabilitative programs, while in prison to understand how I could have done the terrible things I did to Katy. I pray for her and your family daily. It is through these actions, I was able to work through my emotional issues and sought the help that I clearly needed. I understand that you feel I do not have remorse, but I want to express to you that I do.
>
> Through my time incarcerated, I did seek substance abuse treatment and have maintained my sobriety while in prison. Being under the influence of substances when the crime was committed is not an excuse for my actions but was one of the issues I

knew had to be addressed. I sought that help and work daily to remain sober. I plan to continue with maintaining my sobriety, if I am ever released from prison.

After reading McCarthy's 2021 letter and statement, Terry said there was nothing in them that changed her mind. If anything, she said, his first-time mention of the ID confusion, just months after it was revealed in "A Stranger Killed Katy," suggested he was inventing fresh lies.

"I don't think there's any change," Terry said. "But he just keeps plugging along. Each time he goes before the parole board, he thinks, *I've got it licked now. I figured out the key, and this is what they want to hear. So, this is what I'm going to tell them this time, and this is kind of like my last chance.* And then he doesn't get paroled, and then he's got another two years to think, you know, *okay, now I'll come up with another reason.*"

McCarthy's most recent submission to the apology bank, dated May 8, 2022, included a copy of a Mass card signed by Father Buonocore. On its front, next to the shadowy image of a cross, was a line of Scripture: "I am the Resurrection and the Life. John 11:25." Below it, a solemn message read: "The Holy Sacrifice of the Mass will be offered for the repose of the soul of Katherine M. Hawelka," followed by, "With the sympathy of Brian McCarthy."

The accompanying letter read:

> Repository Family,
>
> My name is Brian McCarthy. I have previously submitted letters to the repository for the family of Katherine Hawelka if they chose to read.
>
> In continuation of my heartfelt remorse for my unintentional actions concerning the death of Katherine, I would like you to know of my continual prayers for her during weekly Mass.
>
> Please see the copy of one Mass card said on her behalf.
>
> Respectfully,
>
> Brian McCarthy

Terry also dismissed the Mass card and prayers as insincere, particularly because McCarthy managed to slip in a description of the horrific beating and strangulation of Katy as "unintentional."

"This is what it's like him being a narcissist," Terry said. "He's thinking he can convince people, except, thank God the parole board is not as stupid as he thinks they are, that they would buy this kind of stuff that he's presenting. They've seen enough of it that they realize when somebody's trying to play on them."

Undoubtedly, McCarthy wasn't the first convicted murderer to have a Mass said for his victim. In the Roman Catholic Diocese of Syracuse, for instance, the only restriction on offering a Mass intention is that the person requesting it cannot be running for office.

"Other than that, we believe in forgiveness and prayer. If an individual who harmed another wanted to have a Mass said for the soul of their victim, we would not prohibit it," said Danielle Cummings, director of communications for the Syracuse diocese.

To Terry, the Mass card offered no solace, only another painful reminder of all that McCarthy had taken from Katy and those who loved her. Terry had seen enough of McCarthy to also dismiss the apology letters as his latest attempts to polish his image for the parole board.

"It makes me sad that he's still using my Katy," she said.

Early in 2025, Joe Hawelka Jr. found himself back on the Clarkson University campus for the first time in years. His son had a youth hockey tournament, with games in nearby Norwood and at SUNY Potsdam. On Saturday evening, Clarkson's Division I men's hockey team played archrival St. Lawrence University; Joe and other parents and players attended the home game.

As his son browsed the Clarkson gift shop, looking to buy a shirt, Joe found it unsettling to be there. The bitter memory still lingered of how university officials had initially tried to deflect responsibility for poor campus security—and how its lawyers had even suggested Katy's death was partly her fault. But Joe also remembered how, in the early days of the family's petition, the Clarkson hockey community had rallied behind it, signing in support and encouraging others to oppose McCarthy's parole.

'It's Never Going to End for Us'

Until 2025, the last time Joe had attended a Clarkson hockey game was January 25, 1986. He didn't remember who the team played or who won. He only remembered the fun of being with his sisters, Katy and Carey, along with Katy's classmates. If Brian McCarthy had been there, he never made his presence known. And if he had, Joe was certain neither Katy nor her friends would have had anything to do with him.

In his early victim impact statements, Joe focused on making sure the commissioners understood the heartbreaking details of how McCarthy murdered Katy alongside Walker Arena on the morning of August 29, 1986. But as the years passed, his statements shifted. He found himself pointing out the many ways McCarthy was making up stories to blur the truth, distance himself from responsibility, and shift the narrative in his favor.

"When I read through the minutes from every parole hearing, I am always left with the feeling that he has yet to serve his sentence," Joe said. "Every step of the way he continues to smear the memory of my sister Katy."

Still, Joe took solace in knowing that the parole board had seen through McCarthy's stories, denying his release time and again, calling him out for his lack of credibility and remorse. Joe said he found himself hoping McCarthy, his fiancée, and his attorney continued to file appeals—wasting their time on the same desperate arguments that only reinforced how unrehabilitated he truly was.

As Joe drove back to the hotel after the 2025 Clarkson hockey game, the route took his family past Walker Arena. It was a cold, snowy night, the arena dark and silent. Joe looked at the building and thought: *What a perfect place for an ambush.* He had no doubt that McCarthy had been lying in wait for a victim, watching as students made their way back to campus from downtown. Katy had the tragic misfortune of being spotted by the stranger lurking in the dark.

Joe's visit to Clarkson forced him to confront something he had wrestled with for years: whether he should return to Walker Arena alone and walk the grounds where Katy was attacked. The thought unsettled him. He feared two things: *What if the emotions overwhelmed me?* But also, *what if I felt nothing at all?* In the end, he drove past without stopping, certain he had nothing to gain by searching for answers there. He chose to leave the regret behind.

At the gift shop, Joe watched his son buy a Clarkson hockey sweatshirt as a souvenir of the trip. Someday, Joe decided, he would tell the boy the whole story about Clarkson, about a murder, and about the Aunt Katy he never got to meet.

By February 2025, Katy's brother had begun preparing another impact statement, refocusing on his original goal of making sure the parole board fully grasped the horror of Katy's murder. Reliving the details would not be easy, Joe said, but he was willing to do so, over and over, for as long as it took to keep McCarthy behind bars, and to ensure some other family would never have to endure the long shadow of Katy's killer.

A newspaper "In Memoriam" advertisement placed by Terry Taber in 2006, two decades after the murder of her daughter, Katherine "Katy" Hawelka.

About the Author

William D. LaRue is a former reporter for *The Post-Standard* in Syracuse, New York, and a former online producer for Advance Local's newspaper websites. A native of Potsdam, New York, he earned a bachelor's degree in English from the State University of New York at Potsdam and a master's degree in communications from Syracuse University.

His previous books include *CANDY: True Tales of a 1st Cavalry Soldier in the Korean War and Occupied Japan* (2015), co-written with his father, Kenneth J. LaRue; *Captain Puckett: Sea Stories of a Former Panama Canal Pilot* (2018), co-written with Kenneth P. Puckett; and *A Stranger Killed Katy: The True Story of Katherine Hawelka, Her Murder on a New York Campus, and How Her Family Fought Back* (2021). Through Chestnut Heights Publishing, William also edited and published *The Grocer Who Sold McCarthyism: The Rise and Fall of Anti-Communist Crusader Laurence A. Johnson* (2024) by Fred M. Fiske.

A father of two, William lives in a suburb of Syracuse with his wife, Kathleen.

www.ingramcontent.com/pod-product-compliance
Lightning Source LLC
Chambersburg PA
CBHW070029040426
42333CB00040B/1368